In Search of
Alberto Guerrero

In Search of
Alberto Guerrero

JOHN BECKWITH

Wilfrid Laurier University Press

WLU

We acknowledge the support of the Canada Council for the Arts for our publishing program. We acknowledge the financial support of the Government of Canada through the
Book Publishing Industry Development Program for our publishing activities. This
publication was made possible in part through a generous grant from the Institute for
Canadian Music, Faculty of Music, University of Toronto.

Library and Archives Canada Cataloguing in Publication

Beckwith, John, 1927–
    In search of Alberto Guerrero / John Beckwith.

Includes bibliographical references and index.
ISBN-13: 978-0-88920-496-6
ISBN-10: 0-88920-496-9

    1. Guerrero, Alberto, 1886–1959. 2. Pianists—Canada—Biography. 3. Pianists—
Chile—Biography. 4. Music teachers—Canada—Biography. I. Title.

ML417.G934B39 2006   786.2'092   C2006-901188-5

©2006 Wilfrid Laurier University Press
Waterloo, Ontario, Canada
www.wlupress.wlu.ca

Cover design by P.J. Woodland. Cover image: oil painting of Alberto Guerrero (circa 1940)
by his daughter, Mélisande Irvine. Text design by Catharine Bonas-Taylor.

Printed in Canada

Every reasonable effort has been made to acquire permission for copyright material
used in this text, and to acknowledge all such indebtedness accurately. Any errors and
omissions called to the publisher's attention will be corrected in future printings.

No part of this publication may be reproduced, stored in a retrieval system or transmit-
ted, in any form or by any means, without the prior written consent of the publisher or
a licence from The Canadian Copyright Licensing Agency (Access Copyright). For an
Access Copyright licence, visit www.accesscopyright.ca or call toll free to 1-800-893-5777.

for
Ray Dudley
(1931–2004)

contents

list of illustrations

acknowledgements

Two former Guerrero students, Ray Dudley and William Aide, encouraged me to undertake this study of his life and work. Both have contributed originally to the literature about him, and both helped my project with advice and critical comments on draft sections. A third Guerrero student, Margaret Sheppard Privitello, also encouraged me in the initial stages, and corresponded extensively about his personality and influence. I was saddened to learn of her death in early 2003.

I owe particular thanks to Guerrero's daughter, Mélisande Irvine, who not only donated his papers for study but provided much detailed information in a series of interviews.

In a ten-day visit to Chile in January 2003, I located official documents about Guerrero and his family and interviewed individuals in Santiago and in La Serena (Guerrero's birthplace). Roxana Donoso of the Universidad de Chile library helped with many practical suggestions. Jaime Gómez at the Biblioteca Nacional and Dean Luis Merino Montero of the university's music faculty both drew my attention to relevant articles concerning Guerrero, and Professor Fernando García Arancibia kindly talked with me about his research on Guerrero and his contemporaries, and also led me to further reading. The archdiocesan archives in La Serena pointed me to records about the family.

The translations from Spanish-language sources in the text are all by me. My command of Spanish is limited: while I read the language fairly easily, I neither speak nor write it. By a stroke of exceptionally good luck, Nieves Carrasco attended my talk concerning Guerrero at the University of Toronto on 2 October 2003, and offered to contact Spanish-speaking informants in Chile. She is a Chilean now living in Toronto; her grandfather, the architect Julio Bertrand, belonged to the Grupo de los Diez in the 1910s, along with Guerrero. She has been amazingly resourceful and has contributed hours of work to this enterprise. I was able to pursue the La Serena portions of Guerrero's story through her liaisons with Lidia Escobar, archivist, and Pedro Alvarez, local historian; both have unearthed important verifications concerning the García Guerrero family. Again, through her contacts in Santiago, I obtained, among other valuable items, Guerrero's secondary-school records and some of his early writings for *El Diario ilustrado*. I express here my deep appreciation for Señora Carrasco's interest and active participation in this work.

Esteban Cabezas and Daniel Quiroga, writers for the Santiago newspaper *El Mercurio*, gave me useful elaborations of their Guerrero researches. David Finch, executor of the estate of Myrtle Rose Guerrero, provided details about Guerrero's library. I had lively exchanges with Kevin Bazzana, author of two books about Glenn Gould, and he kindly shared his Hart House program files and other relevant material. I am grateful to Carl Morey of the University of Toronto Faculty of Music, to Suzanne Meyers Sawa of the Faculty of Music library, to Matías Ahumada of the Chilean consulate in Toronto, and to Francesca Bucci, Peter Davis, Kate Galloway, André Leduc, Raffi Kosover, Anna and William McCoy, Ann Morton, Pascal Muzard, Jaime Oxley, Pamela Terry, Kenneth Winters, and my son Larry Beckwith, all of whom responded willingly to requests on special points or provided research assistance. I welcomed, and benefitted from, feedback on early drafts of my text from Larry Beckwith, and from two University of Toronto colleagues, Robin Elliott (Institute for Canadian Music), and the late Geoffrey Payzant (Department of Philosophy). It was on Professor Elliott's initiative that the publication received financial support from the institute, for which I am especially grateful.

In preparing this study, I have been in touch—by letter, by email, and by telephone—with a number of friends and former pupils of Guerrero's, and their input has been enormous. Among them I must mention particularly Alex Champoux, Mary Wilson Dell, Shirley Saul Drager, Stuart Hamilton, Paul Helmer, Sylvia Hunter, Edward Laufer, Bruce Mather, Pierrette LePage Mather, John McIntyre, Colleen Sadler Pohran, R. Murray Schafer, Malcolm Troup, and Ruth Watson Henderson.

To Kathleen McMorrow, my life partner, go warmest thanks for bailing me out of computer problems, suggesting avenues of research (especially from her expertise in early Canadian music periodicals), and commenting constructively on the text in its early stages—and for constant moral support. A reviewer of a former volume by me singled out her index for special commendation. She volunteered, not without a groan, to make another for this volume, for which again she "cannot be lavishly enough thanked."

In the last weeks of 2004, the death of Ray Dudley was a sad blow; he was a splendid versatile performer and devoted Guerrerista. The dedication recalls our lifelong friendship and the many letters and phone calls in which he followed the later progress of this book.

introduction

Near the end of his forty-year career as pianist and teacher in Toronto, Alberto Guerrero was asked for a short autobiographical notice for publicity. "I have no story," he said. The remark suggests long familiarity with, if not wariness of, standard blurbs that describe the winners of "prestigious" or "coveted" awards, who "regularly concertize throughout Europe" or are "among the most sought-after soloists" by "all the leading North American orchestras." Ironic, though evidently not bitter, his response indicates a reluctance to speak about himself and about his work, which in turn may account for the vagueness and confusion that mar most written accounts of his long and active life. Entries under his name in recent musical reference works in Spanish speak at length of his activities as a performer, composer, and intellectual catalyst in his native Chile prior to his departure in 1918, but mention only briefly, and sometimes inaccurately, his later work in the United States and Canada. By contrast, recent Canadian reference works detail his Canadian achievements but merely sketch, again often with errors, his early prominence in the musical life of Chile. Guerrero felt he had no story, and, judging by the scanty surviving documentation of his life, he was content to leave that impression. But everyone has at least one story. In Guerrero's case, it appears, there are, rather, *two* stories.

Under "Guerrero" in the *Encyclopedia of Music in Canada*, readers will find a short article with a portrait and a bibliography of four items, one in Spanish and the rest in English.[1] The bibliography accompanying the entry (also with a portrait) headed "García Guerrero, Alberto" in the *Diccionario de la música española e hispanoamericana*, offers some fifteen titles, all in Spanish.[2] Among them is an abbreviated translation of an obituary tribute from a Canadian journal. The *Encyclopedia* entry mentions Guerrero as composer and refers to three works by title. The *Diccionario* provides a fuller list of his known compositions, in which, however, these three do not appear.

How reliable are these accounts? To examine one biographical issue as it is represented in these entries, we see the problems involved. The *Encyclopedia* claims that Guerrero worked in New York for five years, 1914–19, "as pianist and vocal coach," but the *Diccionario* mentions only that he made a concert tour of "the USA, Canada, and other American countries," around that time. A second example: the *Encyclopedia* refers to Guerrero's early activities in Chile as a conductor, for which scant evidence has emerged. With similar definiteness, the *Diccionario,* covering in two sentences his career in the years 1920–59, establishes him in Toronto as "director of piano studies at the Conservatory of Music of Canada." Guerrero never held an official title in Toronto, although on arriving there he was briefly and unofficially "director of piano studies" at the Hambourg Conservatory. The institution he worked for from 1922 to the end of his life was the Toronto Conservatory of Music, after 1947 called the Royal Conservatory of Music of Toronto. There is no "Conservatory of Music of Canada."

There are reasons for the imprecision of these references. The Chilean musicologist Fernando García Arancibia, author of the *Diccionario* article, drew not only on written histories but on his recollections of conversations with older musicians who had known Guerrero and his brothers. One of his main written sources was an article about the family published by the critic Daniel Quiroga in 1946.[3] Quiroga, now in his eighties, says he was "very young" when he wrote it, and that most of the information came from conversations with the composer Alfonso Leng, a prominent contemporary and close friend of Guerrero's.[4] For both these writers, the lack of documentation, while unfortunate, is understandable. The entry on Guerrero in the *Encyclopedia of Music in Canada* was an in-house production by the writer Mary Willan Mason, who relied on English-language sources such as the Toronto newspaper obituaries of 1959 and the tribute by Boyd Neel published in the Royal Conservatory *Monthly Bulletin* the following year, whose inaccuracies she had no reason to suspect.[5]

That his most notable pupil was Glenn Gould—a point of only passing mention in the Spanish dictionary entry—became the main theme of North American and European journalistic and lexicographical comments about Guerrero in recent decades. Reporting on a Toronto symposium of former Guerrero students in 1990, William Littler of the Toronto *Star* began his article:

> [Guerrero] founded and conducted Santiago's first symphony orchestra, was one of the Chilean city's most prominent critics, taught some of its

leading composers and introduced its citizens to the music of Debussy and Ravel, none of which would be of the slightest interest to us today were it not for a fellow pianist by the name of Glenn Gould. In addition to all these accomplishments, you see, Alberto Guerrero bears the distinction of having been the principal teacher of the greatest pianist Canada has ever produced.[6]

The item's headline, "Remembering Man Who Taught Glenn Gould," confirmed that, in the *Star*'s view, Guerrero indeed had "no story," or at least none that was unconnected with the world-renowned pupil of his later years—music annals at large, whether Chilean or Canadian, be damned. You see (or you *will* see, at any rate), Littler's summary of Guerrero's Chilean years is wholly derivative and, like its sources, at least partly wrong— again for understandable, if unfortunate, reasons.

In the many writings and interviews of his mature years, Gould himself spoke of Guerrero not by name but as "my teacher." (Their evident divergence of views in the 1950s forms an intriguing part of the "story," to be dealt with later.) Guerrero was also my teacher; I speak of him as "Guerrero," and always spoke *to* him as "*Mister* Guerrero." (To the receptionists at the Royal Conservatory when I was a student, he was "*Señor* Guerrero"—which they pronounced *Senior*.) He was the most powerful influence in my musical education. I have spoken about him often, thought of him more often, and have responded on several occasions to opportunities and invitations to write concerning him—from an obituary notice in 1959 for the *Canadian Music Journal* (not without its own mistakes, I must now acknowledge) to a brief piece forty years later for the "great piano teachers" column of the British magazine *Piano*.[7] In 2002, his daughter, Mélisande Irvine, donated a collection of clippings, photos, letters, and other documents, mainly relating to his career in the 1920s and '30s, to the Faculty of Music library at the University of Toronto. A preliminary scan of this material, followed by discussion with a few colleagues, encouraged me to attempt a fuller Guerrero "story," to search for a more rounded (and, I hoped, more accurate) record of the life and work of this remarkably influential and well-loved man. Perhaps what seemed like two very separate stories—the Chilean one and the Canadian one—could be made to connect.

In a word, I hoped to make Guerrero less of a shadow. A shadow is all that is left of his many inspiring performances, since virtually none survives in recordings. A shadow is how he is characterized in the vast literature surrounding Glenn Gould, almost without exception. Again, a shadow is what remains of his achievement for anyone who, in early 2004, consulted the online *New Grove Dictionary*: his name turns up, either as "Alberto Guerrero" or as "Alberto García Guerrero," in a random search of seven individual articles (the main entry "Chile" and six biographical entries), but you will not find him listed in the index.[8]

If the story has two parts, my narration itself takes two tones—part objective research and part personal memoir. This is probably inevitable: I knew Guerrero personally, but only during his last years. I trust the resulting shifts of view now and then do not unduly upset the consistency and flow of the text. In the course of my search, I have often had moments of regret that someone (I or another writer) had not begun twenty-five or thirty years earlier, when key players in Guerrero's life were still around. His motives in abandoning composition, in avoiding documentation of his major literary projects or recordings of his principal performances, above all in "burning his bridges" by leaving Chile for faraway Canada, remain elusive.

So, while the various open questions about Guerrero's career may have formed the goal of my study, I realize I have attained definitive answers only in partial and tentative ways. In the almost complete absence of personal diaries and letters, and given the conflicting versions of many details, the search has been demanding. Nevertheless, it has produced, I believe, a fuller and more appropriate view of the events of his life than was previously available. I will welcome corrections and (especially) additional documented information to add to the story.

one

Chile / Canada

Alberto Guerrero (1886–1959) spent his early life, until the age of thirty-two, in his native Chile, and his later years in Canada. The two countries lie a vast distance apart at the northern and southern outer extremities of the Western Hemisphere, and have had until late in the twentieth century minimal exchange. In 1918, when Guerrero arrived in Toronto, the city which was to be his permanent home, there were virtually no other Chileans living there. The Chilean consulate in Toronto came into permanent existence only in the late 1970s; Guerrero himself served as Chilean "honorary consul" from 1921 through 1928, and again intermittently during the late 1930s, with evidently only light duties.

But the two countries have a number of features in common: Chile occupies a narrow strip 4,300 kilometres in length between the Andes mountains and the Pacific, its population concentrated in the metropolis of Santiago and a few smaller, widely separated cities. Its history is a complex mix of native and colonial characters and events. Colonial cultural attitudes persisted following independence, which dates from the second decade of the nineteenth century. Chile is Canada placed on end.

Much of Canada's population is concentrated in half a dozen mega-cities wide distances apart, along a narrow strip 5,500 kilometres long between the American border and the far north. Encounters between First Nations and colonial powers mark its history, and colonial attitudes lingering from the rebellions of the 1830s led one critic to characterize it as a cultural "bush garden."[1] Canada is Chile laid on its side.

From several standpoints, then, it makes sense that Guerrero felt at home in Canada. That he never returned to Chile, even for a short visit to relatives and colleagues, is both remarkable and puzzling. In the first years of his "exile," he received, according to several accounts, invitations—offers of major positions in Chilean education and the arts—but always turned them down. The late 1920s and early 1930s were a period of rapid flowering in Chile, with the establishment of university departments and other institutions bringing a new strength to the national cultural reform movements with which Guerrero had been identified in the 1910s. But, his daughter recollects, he feared the "politics" that would ensue if he were to accept a role there.[2]

He evidently referred to *cultural* politics—the familiar in-fighting and power plays of intellectual and artistic group efforts. These he viewed as a waste of time better spent on performance, creativity, and study. But was he thinking also of the political scene in Chilean society more generally? In this respect Chile throughout his lifetime presented a far less stable picture than Canada: in the 1880s, the decade of his birth, Chileans suffered through a severe border conflict with Peru and Bolivia, known as the War of the Pacific. Although Canada participated in a succession of foreign wars from the late nineteenth century through the mid-twentieth, its government was peaceful—free from the civil outbursts, frontier clashes, and dictatorial regimes that repeatedly interrupted life in Chile.

Guerrero came to know the length and breadth of Canada better than he ever knew the length and breadth of Chile. His concert engagements as a young musician took place in four or five Chilean centres—principally Santiago, but sometimes the port of Valparaíso and its resort-town twin Viña del Mar, or the smaller centre of Concepción to the south, or his home town of La Serena to the north. There is evidence of one significant visit to Punta Arenas, the country's southernmost community. In Canada he came to know all the main geographic regions—not so much from concert touring as from his travels as an examiner for the Toronto (later Royal) Conservatory of Music. These occupied him in the late spring annually from the middle 1920s to the early 1950s, and brought him into contact with teachers and performers from coast to coast, often including small towns in (for example) the British Columbia interior, or the Prairie provinces, or northern New Brunswick. Though his roots were Chilean, he acquired a deeper appreciation and knowledge of his adopted country than have many Canadian-born citizens.

Beginnings in La Serena

La Serena, located 470 kilometres north of Santiago and twelve kilometres inland from the Bay of Coquimbo in Chile's "near north," is the second oldest city in the country, after Santiago; it was founded in 1544. Destroyed shortly afterwards in a war with the resident Indigenous people, it was immediately rebuilt under Governor Francisco de Aguirre along traditional Spanish-colonial lines, and today retains its pleasant palm-lined Plaza de Armas, a cathedral, and several parish churches from the seventeenth and eighteenth centuries. The town's growth into a thriving centre for silver and copper mining dates from the early nineteenth century; the region supported at that period "a flourishing number of foundries."[3] A short tram line connects La Serena to the Pacific port of Coquimbo, with its busy marine traffic and attractive beaches. In 1885, the year before Alberto Guerrero's birth, the population of La Serena was just over 17,000. (The population in 2000 was approximately 120,000.)

In a birth certificate dated "district no. 1, department of La Serena, 5 March 1886," his father, described as "Daniel García y Urriondo [sic], Chilean, forty-five years old, inspector general," declares that "in his home in the Calle de Infante [sic], on 6 February last, at six o'clock in the morning, was born a child of the masculine sex, legitimate son of the declarant and of his wife, Doña Nicolasa Guerrero y Carvajal, Chilean, forty-one years old, devoted to the occupations of her sex, and this child they have named Antonio Alberto." The certificate bears the signatures of Daniel García and two witnesses.

Juan Daniel García Uriondo was the natural son of Pedro Antonio García and Rosario Uriondo; he was baptized in La Merced parish in La Serena on 3 February 1841, aged two months—indicating that he was born in early December of 1840. That both parents are named in the baptismal record is an indication that the birth was "recognized": for most illegitimate births, only the mother's name would be given (the couple had at least one other child). The term "ensayador general" ("inspector general") suggests that Daniel was a mining engineer, and that he graduated with the title "ensayador" from a mining course either in La Serena or in the larger school in Copiapó, to the north.[4] His reputed wealth may have been based on mining investments during that buoyant period in the development of northern Chile.

If precise data on Daniel is skimpy, that concerning his wife, Nicolasa Guerrero, is practically non-existent. In his later career Alberto adopted her surname, Guerrero, rather than his father's, García, which would have been more conventional. This has been interpreted as a sign that he was more devoted to his mother than to his father, but, as we will see, he hardly knew his father. Some biographical notices actually omit the father's name and refer to him only as the son of Nicolasa. Another detail: most notices give his baptismal names in reverse order to those on the actual certificate.

Both parents were approaching middle age when Guerrero was born. He was the second youngest of a large family. His oldest brother, Daniel, was nineteen years his senior, having been born at La Serena in 1867. The children appear in local records in La Serena as follows:

– Daniel Aristides Ramón, born 30 August 1867
– María Luisa, born 1 March 1872
– María Elena, born 27 April 1875
– Carmen Victoria Inés, born 20 January, baptized 25 January, 1881;
– Nicolás Eduardo, born 17 July, baptized 19 July, 1883;
– Antonio Alberto, born 6 February, baptized 12 February, 1886;
– Amelia, born 30 May, baptized 5 June, 1887.

Guerrero's daughter recalls another uncle, Carlos, and an aunt, Rosa; their dates of birth are so far not located, but should place them among the older siblings. The records may be incomplete; the family may have moved away from La Serena, perhaps to Copiapó, and then back again. In any case, it appears Alberto belonged to a large family. His brothers Daniel and Eduardo had especially close relationships with him, and the trio of "los hermanos García Guerrero" came to figure prominently in Chilean artistic annals. Of the sisters, Ms. Irvine recalls that the closest in her father's affections was Amelia. She was also the only sister who married; the others remained single. Ms. Irvine says that as a youngster she was introduced to several of the aunts at the villa near Valparaíso of her uncle, Dr. Daniel García Guerrero.[5]

It was a well-to-do and cultured family. Nicolasa, a skilled pianist, was the children's music teacher. The oldest son, Daniel, showed special musical aptitude, and Alberto received his childhood piano lessons from him as well as from his mother. Two professional musicians are known to have been active in La Serena in the late 1800s, a Señor Manfredi and a Señor Calixto Valenzuela. Manfredi was "profesor de canto" at the Liceo de Hombres, the public school attended by Alberto's older brothers. He also taught at the Escuela Normal and the Seminario Conciliar, and played both violin and piano. Valenzuela maintained a private teaching studio and was also director of the Banda de Música de La Serena y Coquimbo.[6] It is possible that the García Guerrero children went to one or other or both of these individuals for more advanced instruction in music. The common understanding however is that Alberto did not, and that he was an autodidact apart from the lessons with his mother and older brother: the claim is in many respects extraordinary.[7]

Towards the end of his life, Guerrero made oblique reference to his upbringing in a typically wry remark to Sylvia Hunter: "I had a lesson once," he said, "but I didn't like it."[8]

We lack precise evidence regarding his mother's pianistic formation and abilities. Of the brother, Daniel, it is said that during his years in medical practice in Santiago and Valparaíso he was an avid and accomplished musical dilletante, playing the solo part in a Mendelssohn piano concerto with an amateur orchestra, and making "frequent trips" to Europe, bringing back the latest published scores.[9] Whether the young Alberto accompanied him on such trips is not known.

The music critic Kenneth Winters, who produced a radio documentary in 1996 about Guerrero the teacher, said he sought in vain an answer to the question, "who was *Guerrero's* teacher?" The same Chilean sources who describe Guerrero as self-educated in music also recount that in childhood he already showed exceptional gifts as a pianist, and that later he developed a command of harmony, counterpoint, and composition sufficient to produce five works for the lyric stage, as well as chamber works, songs, piano solos, and possibly some pieces for orchestra—making Winters's question a reasonable one to ask: was all this really possible without professional guidance, without a formal program of instruction? Guerrero apparently did not enrol in the Conservatorio Nacional; the music department of the Universidad de Chile fine arts faculty came into existence only in the early 1930s; and his early-blossoming talent did not attract the kind of public sponsorship that enabled his young compatriot Claudio Arrau, seventeen years Guerrero's junior, to work with leading teachers in Europe. But if his only teachers were Nicolasa and Daniel, a further reasonable question (as Winters also asks) is, "Who taught *them*?"[10] This is one of the many elements in the Guerrero story where further investigation is called for.

Two close colleagues, Alfonso Leng and Domingo Santa Cruz (who appear later in this account), were students of Enrique Soro, composition teacher at the Conservatorio in Santiago, but whether Guerrero was also, again there is no solid evidence.

His daughter recalls the respect Guerrero often voiced for the pianist Ricardo Viñes, but there is no indication that he ever met Viñes personally.[11] Viñes's years of residence in South America, including extended periods in Chile, came after Guerrero left the country, making it doubtful that Guerrero ever went to him for lessons. Similarly, the possibility of lessons with Isidor Philipp in Paris, or later in Montreal, is raised in recent explorations of Guerrero's story by Kevin Bazzana, Sylvia Hunter, and others.[12] Guerrero may have attended master classes or had one or two sessions of private instruction with Philipp in Paris during his summer visits in the 1920s and '30s, or in Montreal during Philipp's short residencies there in the 1940s; however, if verified, this would suggest only a supplement to his by-then long-fulfilled pianistic formation. Thoroughly remarkable though it is, the claim of his self-education in music may be true after all.

Although we do not know a lot about Guerrero's education, we know he was not a typical Catholic of his generation. In the early twenty-first century, three out of four Chileans were Roman Catholic; in the late nineteenth and early twentieth centuries the majority was much higher, more like nine out of ten. There is evidence that Alberto Guerrero's older siblings were educated in the public schools of La Serena, the boys at the Liceo de Hombres, the girls at the Liceo de Niñas.[13] Guerrero's aunt, Carmen García Uriondo, was the founding director of the Liceo de Niñas, and her son, Guerrero's cousin, became "intendente y administrador" of the schools.[14] Their curricula, though no doubt embracing features of the overwhelmingly dominant faith, were non-sectarian. Associates in his adult life gathered that, as the youngest son, Alberto was (by custom) expected to enter the priesthood, and that in early youth he even began serious studies to that end.[15] This evidently incorrect impression may have been merely a reflection of his broad knowledge and of the respect he retained for the Church even as an agnostic. Studies at the Liceo covered the classical program of arts and sciences (including music, with Señor Manfredi), rather than preparations for the religious vocation, such as might have been expected at a Catholic seminary. From what we know of the achievements of Daniel, Eduardo, and Alberto García Guerrero, their early education was thorough and humanist. Besides the musical and literary contributions of all three, Daniel and Eduardo both became leading professionals and university educators, the former in medicine and the latter in law.

A local newspaper item of September 1892 announces a sudden and fundamental interruption in the family:

> The much-respected Don Daniel García Uriondo has died in Santiago.
>
> Señor García, possessor of a powerful intelligence and profound abilities in the natural sciences, was an enterprising and progressive industrialist who contributed tremendously to the development of mining in Coquimbo province. A distinguished metallurgist, he was responsible for several undertakings in this field, by which modern and improved methods were introduced, to the benefit of silver mining at the Arqueros mines.
>
> Señor García has died young and when there was still much to hope for from his intelligence and his enterprising and progressive spirit.[16]

Guerrero's father was fifty-one years of age. The younger Daniel was now in charge of the large family, and at length they relocated in Santiago. Prior to their father's death, the García Guerreros had clearly established periodic contact with the capital through visits; this is suggested by, among other evidence, Alberto's childhood memories of opera performances he was taken to. According to the obituary notice, his father died there. One writer gives 1912 as the date of the relocation; another says it occurred "in the first decade of the twentieth century."[17] But evidence points to an even earlier date: the period from 1895 to 1910 saw a remarkable expansion of the city, and growth of the prosperous new Providencia neighborhood, in which the Garcías were likely participants. At age fourteen Alberto was enrolled in the Instituto Nacional, Santiago's leading public secondary school.

His examination reports for December 1900 and December 1901 confirm him in an academic program that covered, in the first year, French, Castillian (i.e., Spanish), mathematics, history, geography, and natural sciences, and in the second year the same subjects plus German. His grades appear good, though not exceptional. The Instituto was, and is, noted for its high scholastic entrance standards.[18] From one biographical source we learn that Guerrero "received his education at the Barros Arana Academy."[19] The Internado Nacional Barros Arana was founded in 1902, and it appears that Alberto enrolled there in the founding year. An "internado" is a resident *liceo* or high school; the Instituto Nacional also took boarders.[20] Thus, unlike his older brothers and sisters, Alberto received the later part of his schooling in Santiago and not in La Serena, and, though he may have made public appearances as a pianist in the La Serena years, it seems clear that it was in the more cosmopolitan centre that his musical talents emerged.

Young Pianist, Young Composer

On completing his *liceo* studies, Alberto did not follow his older brothers, despite their evident urgings, into an academic or professional post-secondary program. The call of music was too strong. By his late teens, he had mastered a great deal of the advanced standard repertoire for piano, and had begun to compose, both in the conventional light-music forms of his time and place and in more adventurous idioms suggested by his study of newer pieces as they appeared from European publishers. His intellectual curiosity had immersed him in the theoretical writings of contemporaries such as Hugo Riemann and Vincent D'Indy.[21] By the age of nineteen or twenty he began to experience the worlds of journalism and music theatre.

Among remnants of Guerrero's personal library are copies of standard treatises published in the early 1900s, from which, it is reasonable to assume, he pursued his program of self-education at this time. They include Vincent d'Indy's two-volume *Cours de composition musicale;* harmony texts by Henri Reber, Théodore Dubois, and François-Auguste Gevaert; the latter's *Nouveau traité d'instrumentation* in both French and Spanish; a Spanish translation of Charles-Marie Widor's manual on orchestration, based on Berlioz; the two-volume *Histoire de la musique* of Jules Combarieu; and Hugo Riemann's analyses of J.S. Bach's *Wohltemperiertes Clavier.*[22]

A Chilean "who's who" of the 1920s summarizes the varied directions of his early career: by 1905 he was active in musical theatre, his compositions showed modernity and originality, he was a music critic for one of the leading dailies, and he was becoming known as a musical performer—and in every area he appeared "a winner (*triunfador*)."[23]

The first sphere mentioned is theatre, where, the summary says, Guerrero "asomó su arte por las bambalinas"—specifying backstage involvement ("bambalinas" refers to overhead scenery): does this imply tasks beyond those of a resident composer? For example, was he also a rehearsal keyboardist? July 1908 saw the première of his one-act operetta *Rucacahuiñ,* described as a "zarzuela de costumbres araucanas," in two scenes with a musical intermezzo. The libretto was by the dramatist and impresario Aurelio Díaz Meza (1879–1933). The indication "on Araucanian customs" (or "in the Araucanian manner") suggests that both composer and writer were attracted by the pre-contact history of Chile. Araucanía was an indigenous culture centred in the territory around Temuco, just south of Concepción. A publication of Díaz Meza's in 1907 bears the title *En la Araucanía.* He and Guerrero were later to collaborate on at least three, perhaps four, further stage works—none of the music has survived. (I discuss these works, and Guerrero's youthful critiques for *El Diario ilustrado,* later).

Busy with group activities in theatre and in journalism—and, as we will see, in various reform and avant-garde artistic movements—Guerrero was simultaneously isolating himself in those years to polish his pianism towards its most virtuosic extent. In 1912 he presented two solo recitals in Valparaíso's Teatro Colón (14 June and 27 July), in which he executed extremely demanding programs with apparently sensational success. The first of these began with Balakirev's "oriental fantasy" *Islamey,* still regarded as a sort of technical Everest for pianists. It continued with works by Liszt (*Legend no. 2, St. Francis of Padua Walking on the Water; Liebestraum; Tarantella di bravura,* after Auber's *La muette de Portici*) and Chopin (Waltz, Opus 34, no. 1; Études, Opus 10, no. 5, and Opus 25, nos. 1 and 9), as well as Debussy's *En bâteau,* a *Moment Musical* by Moritz Moszkowski, and a piano transcription of Théodore Dubois's symphonic poem *Les Abeilles.* Encores were another major Liszt work, the *Sonnet 104 of Petrarch,* and Guerrero's own *Capricho.*

For the July concert the program was equally virtuosic: Schumann's *Études symphoniques* were followed by more Liszt and Chopin: Liszt's

Alberto García Guerrero, "the young pianist": photo ca. 1915 (Sociedad Chilena del Derecho de Autor); caricature, artist unknown, same period (Faculty of Music library, University of Toronto, Guerrero Collection)

Hungarian Rhapsody no. 10 and Chopin's Ballade no. 3 in A flat, Opus 47, and Étude in E, Opus 10, no. 3. Other works were Grieg's *Wedding Day at Troldhaugen*, Opus 65, no. 6; *Automne* (Concert étude, Opus 35, no. 2) by Cécile Chaminade; and Carl Tausig's Valse-Caprice, after Johann Strauss's *Man lebt nur einmal*.

The two concerts may have been repeated in Santiago at the Teatro Municipal. Together they had a resounding effect, immediately elevating Guerrero to a major position in professional music circles in Chile, according to contemporaries.[24] The press comments convey the sense of occasion: "the large and distinguished audience, which filled the hall, applauded spontaneously and warmly"; "the most brilliant artistic and social success." For the second concert, mention of the "social" factor was elaborated: "a select gathering which filled the vast expanses of the elegant Teatro Colón"; "one noticed in the boxes the splendid dresses of our most elegant ladies." But, the anonymous reviewer added, "the artistic success of the evening was all that might be hoped from a master like García Guerrero, who earned warm critical approbation on his previous appearance here." For both concerts, the performances elicited superlatives: "His bearing (*apostura*) is straightforward and correct, his execution clear and most precise"; "a complete artist"; "programming beyond criticism" (*intachable*); "superbly done"; "impeccably realized"; "exquisite delicacy"; "refined sensibility"; "stupendous brilliance."[25]

Through his friendship with a fellow composer, Alfonso Leng, Guerrero was engaged in the same season as pianist for concerts with a piano trio, in collaboration with Leng as cellist and Humberto Busenius as violinist, within the framework of the Academia Musical Ortiz de Zárate, in which his brother Eduardo was a leading light.

The following year, 1913, he appeared with Eduardo in a lecture-recital on the music of Franz Liszt. Presented again at the Colón in Valparaíso, on 13 February, this was the first of several popular lectures devoted to European instrumental repertoire then largely unfamiliar to Chilean audiences, the texts delivered by Eduardo and the piano illustrations played by Alberto. On this inaugural occasion, Eduardo's discourse was divided into sections devoted in turn to "Liszt as composer," "Liszt as pianist," and "Liszt's artistic propaganda." Alberto's interspersed performances were *St. Francis of Padua Walking on the Water; Liebestraum;* the Concert Étude no. 2, *La leggierezza;* the Hungarian Rhapsodies nos. 11 and 12; and the Polonaise no. 2 in E. The reviewers saluted Guerrero as "an artist of major talent with an admirable mastery of performance"; they insisted, "We knew Señor García Guerrero as a Chopin player, and if he earned our high praise in that romantic repertoire, as an interpreter of Liszt he has earned much more." An undated review, evidently from later the same year, records a second lecture-recital, this time given in Santiago and devoted to Robert Schumann. Alberto's contribution consisted of the *Études symphoniques;* the *Arabesque;* a "Nocturne" (the *Nachtstück,* Opus 23?); and *Carnaval.* Again the press reacted with superlatives to "an event which we will remember for a long time, since the admirable talent of these young artists leaves an impression that is anything but superficial"; "The pianist was magnificent in the execution of this program. His name resounds daily in our artistic circles as a virtuoso of special agreeableness (*dulzura*), the poetic quality of whose interpretations easily wins public approval."[26]

In later years these events were often recalled as having had a decisive impact on musical taste in the country. Chopin, Wagner, Paganini, and MacDowell were among other composers whose works were explored and expounded.[27] Though their music was widely known elsewhere, it had been little cultivated until then by Chileans, whose musical enthusiasms were concentrated on opera, especially of the Italian school.

The music historian Robert Stevenson indeed speaks of a "vassalage to Italy" felt in Chilean musical circles at the turn of the century, while Juan Pablo González, musicologist at Santiago's Universidad Católica, finds a cultural "dichotomy" in the period—a large segment of the musical public favouring opera and a smaller elite favouring instrumental concert music, especially by the newer composers.[28] There was no regular symphonic

Program, lecture by Eduardo García Guerrero, with piano illustrations by Alberto García Guerrero. Teatro Colón, Valparaíso, 13 February 1913 (Guerrero Collection)

orchestra in the capital, and the first cycle of the Beethoven symphonies, given in 1914 by an orchestra organized specifically for the purpose, is still referred to as a historic breakthrough. The conductor was Nino Marcelli. Guerrero was in later life credited by some commentators with having founded and conducted an orchestra in Chile around this time, but the claim is false. In those years, players in the local opera orchestra and in the pit bands of the new *biógrafos* (silent-movie theatres) would be conscripted for special concert performances. In the same season as the Beethoven-symphonies venture, the Dutch cellist Michael Penha, a recent arrival on the Chilean scene, announced a cycle of concerts at the Teatro Unión Central by a "Sociedad de conciertos sinfónicos," for which he would conduct and/or appear as soloist. The following season, 1915, there was an even more ambitious series conducted by Eliodoro Ortiz de Zárate. These subscription offerings did not yet coalesce into a permanent symphonic organization. Interestingly, Penha's society announces in the local press a concert for 11 July 1914 featuring "a large orchestra conducted by the distinguished maestro Señor Alberto García Guerrero."[29] A later bulletin states that "many of the society's subscribers have requested Señor Michel [*sic*] Penha to delay his concert for a few days, since some of them are suffering from illness. Acceding to their wishes, Señor Penha has postponed the event until further notice."[30] It is not known when, or if, the postponed concert took place. Its program was to include works by Schubert, Lalo, Grieg, Bruch, Saint-Saens, and Boëllmann; though titles are not given, the group of names suggests that Penha was to appear as soloist in several numbers. Active performers, as both Penha and Guerrero were at this time, are sometimes called on to assume conducting duties. This bit of evidence suggests that in his Santiago years Guerrero did so on a few occasions—and no doubt with efficiency and distinction. It does not however mean that he considered emphasizing conducting over other musical tasks or ever regarded himself as "a conductor" in a career sense.

The young professional musicians in his circle appear to have reacted to the prevailing artistic climate by putting their energies into informal groups for study and performance, and (wherever possible) propagandizing on behalf of a broader repertoire, newer works, and, of course, their own productions. Years later, the composer Acario Cotapos (1889–1969) recalled the atmosphere in Santiago in 1915 and the group's motives:

> We were a group of musicians—Alfonso Leng, Carlos Lavín, and Alberto García Guerrero—living in a sort of musical sanctuary from which as yet we had no wings to fly. We were a small nest of composers living through the tremendous events of the First World War and the echoes, equally significant, of the music which Stravinsky, Ravel, and the distant monster Schoenberg were starting to create, which threatened us with its unheard and unimagined new forms.[31]

Throughout his life, Guerrero was associated with small audiences, often in someone's front parlour, and a new or seldom-cultivated repertoire. At the same time, he seemed never to want to isolate himself from the larger musical public: the operetta productions were a popular sphere, his early solo programs had catholic appeal, the Penha venture was widely publicized, and his brother Eduardo's lectures drew large attendance.

Further trio concerts occupied Guerrero in the 1914 and '15 seasons, this time with Armando Carvajal, concertmaster of the opera orchestra at the Teatro Municipal, as violinist and Michael Penha as cellist.[32] The trio is reported to have presented "magnificent" performances of major works from the standard piano-trio literature, in Santiago as well as in other main cities of Chile: Valparaíso, Constitución, Concepción, Valdivia, and Puerto Montt.[33] The programs of their cycle of four concerts at the Teatro Dieciocho, Santiago, in May and June 1915, covered a broad gamut:

14 May:
Jean Huré: Trio no. 1 (1907)
(piano solos) Ravel: *Jeux d'eau;* Debussy: *L'isle joyeuse*
Chaikovski: Trio Opus 50

28 May:
Beethoven: Trio Opus 97 in B flat (*Archduke*)
(violin and piano) Mendelssohn: Andante from Concerto in e
Mendelssohn: Trio no. 2 in c, Opus 66

11 June:
(violin and piano) César Franck: Sonata in A
(piano solo) Franck: Prelude, Chorale, and Fugue
Franck: Trio in E [?][34]

25 June:
Schumann: Trio no. 2 in F, Opus 80
(cello and piano) Schumann: Adagio and Allegro, Opus 70 (originally for
horn and piano)
Brahms: Trio no. 3 in c, Opus 101.

The contemporary works by Huré, Ravel, and Debussy were distinctly
innovative. Schumann, Brahms, and the then-seldom-played Franck all
represented advances in repertoire over earlier chamber-music efforts in
Chile. Guerrero's performance of the Prelude, Chorale, and Fugue was
described as "a brilliant and fully understood interpretation"; this work
became a staple of his repertoire in the years to come.

As a teacher of composition, Guerrero is repeatedly acknowledged
by his contemporaries in Chile. In this period he also evidently began
teaching piano performance, which became the dominant specialty of his
later career in Canada. After describing his influence on young composers,
a tribute by his friend Alfonso Leng acknowledges Guerrero's pedagogy by
noting that "in the teaching of the piano, an instrument whose most elusive secrets he understood, he evolved...his own system."[35] Guerrero
always resisted the idea of a method or system of teaching; Leng's remark
may have simply meant that he followed no standard pedagogical con-
vention. The two outstandingly talented Chilean pianists in the early years
of the twentieth century, both youthful prodigies, were Rosita Renard
(1894–1949) and Claudio Arrau (1903–91). Renard left the country in
1910 for a period of study and concert-giving in Germany, but returned to
Chile after a few years and is said to have studied (1915) with Guerrero.[36]
Arrau gave his first public concert at the age of five; two years later he too
went to Germany for further musical study, and resumed regular contact
with Chilean musical life starting only in 1922, after Guerrero's departure.
Later, during his several visits to Canada, Arrau formed a warm friendship
with his older compatriot.

The piano is a constant factor in the steady stream of instrumental compositions Guerrero produced alongside his stage works. The list includes
works for piano solo (*Con moto*, 1906; *Tempo di vals*, 1907; *Vals triste*,
n.d.; *Capricho*, 1912) and for the duo of cello and piano (*Danse*, n.d.;
Chants oubliés, 1916).[37] One movement of a quintet for piano and strings
is preserved, thirteen pages in length, dated 1910. Single movements for
piano solo, complete though undated and unsigned, also exist—an "Allegro" of two pages and a "Final" of nine pages—perhaps intended for a
longer cyclic form such as a sonata. There is also an undated "Minué," for
string orchestra, a piece in ABA form following more or less the conven-
tion of the "modo antico" familiar from Chaikovski's *Mozartiana* and

Grieg's *Suite from Holberg's Time*. Of the *Vals triste* Hans Lach wrote that: "It is the most refined and distinguished [example] of its genre," and "reveals already an aristocratic and elegant artist who puts forward his inspirations in a rich and personal harmonic format."[38] *Chants oubliés*—dated "New York, August 1916" and dedicated to Michael Penha—came to be frequently featured in his concerts with that artist.

Whatever the lost stage-music scores may reveal if they are ever located, these instrumental works show Guerrero striving for new and unconventional harmonies such as those he was encountering as a performer in the works of Scriabin, Scott, Ravel, and Schoenberg. The little *Con moto* already covers in a few bars unexpected reaches of modulation. The manuscript of *Tempo di vals* suggests a process of serious thought by its pencil and ink reworkings—more than might be anticipated in a short work in dance idiom. The more fully blown *Danse* exhibits high-register whole-tone passages for the cello and whole-tone clusters for the piano. The impressionism of Debussy and Ravel is further evoked as a model for the *Chants oubliés*. In the *Vals triste* the tension and obliqueness of the harmonies refer more closely to Scriabin. The same may be said of the short song, *To Maud Allan*, composed in New York in 1916 to an English-language poem by Witter Bynner.[39]

A Composer for the Stage

Nineteenth-century musical life in Santiago centred on opera; a significant opera season also took place each year in Valparaíso. There was no permanent orchestra apart from the opera orchestra, and little choral or chamber-music cultivation; the Conservatorio Nacional, the only arena of professional musical education, concentrated on preparing singers and instrumentalists for careers in the opera world. Although this sometimes leads historians to depict the musical milieu as backward, the operatic scene itself was lively, venturesome, and remarkably cosmopolitan. The repertoire was largely Italian, but included occasional works in German—Wagner's *Tannhäuser* and *Parsifal*—and French—Meyerbeer's *L'Africaine* and *Les Huguenots*, Gounod's *Faust*.[40] Sometimes the gap between the European world première and the Chilean première was surprisingly short: examples are *Falstaff* (1893, 1896) and *La Bohème* (1896, 1898). *Pagliacci* (1892) and *Manon Lescaut* (1893) were both mounted in Santiago before 1900; *Madama Butterfly* (1904) before 1910; *La Fanciulla del West* (1910) and *Il Trittico* (1918) before 1920. Celebrity artists from Europe appeared on the Santiago stage; examples from the period of Guerrero's youth are Luisa Tetrazzini as Elisabeth in *Tannhäuser* and Mimi in *La Bohème* and a *Rigoletto* with Tito Schipa in the title role and Amelita Galli-Curci as

Gilda. Pietro Mascagni was a guest conductor in 1911.[41] The geographical isolation of Chile presented no major barrier to such cultural enterprise. The orchestra, chorus, and production personnel were all Chilean-based, but soloists were often engaged on a circuit that included the established houses in Buenos Aires and Lima. Of special significance was the first production of an opera by a Chilean composer, Eliodoro Ortiz de Zárate's *La florista de Lugano* (1895). Its libretto was in Italian, not Spanish; an earlier work by the same composer had received a première at La Scala in Milan.

The García Guerrero family's musical interests clearly included opera-going. In later years, Alberto Guerrero both knew and loved a great deal of operatic literature. Having grown up with exposure to the standard operas, his musical imagination often suggested dramatic dimensions. For example, he would interpret an instrumental slow movement by Mozart as a sort of solo aria, its punctuating phrases representing the chorus's interpolated comments ("yes, you are right; yes, that is so"). The development section in Chopin's Sonata in b, Opus 58, was "operatic" in a different sense: its tortuous chromaticism and disjointedness, he found, anticipated Wagner. I was struck when once, in a lesson, he recalled the "wonderful fourth act" of *Les Huguenots,* a formerly popular work seldom mounted in the twentieth century; on another occasion he described the cultural sensation when *La Bohème* hit Santiago and people whistled Musetta's waltz-song at every street corner. These were memories from his childhood, and it is no surprise that his early compositional energies found their main outlet in works for the lyric stage.

In fact, from various sources, there is evidence that Guerrero was responsible for five musical scores in the light-opera genre. The titles are: *Rucacahuiñ, El Copihue, Damas de Moda, Jefe de Familia,* and *Mariposa.* Production details are known for only two of these pieces: *Rucacahuiñ* was first given in 1908 at the (now defunct) Teatro Edén, Santiago; *Damas de Moda* received its première in 1914, at an unnamed location. Both works have libretti by a well-known Chilean writer, Aurelio Díaz Meza;[42] that for *Damas de Moda* was published in Santiago in the year of its première, and that for *Rucacahuiñ* some years later in the "fortnightly review" *Mundo Teatral.*[43] The published book for *Damas de Moda* offers a list of other theatrical works by Díaz Meza, from which it appears that he was also the librettist of the zarzuela *Jefe de Familia* ("Head of the family," one act, three scenes), and the three-act operetta *Mariposa;* for both, the acknowledged composer is "Maestro Alberto García Guerrero." The last-named work is described as "en preparación," so it may not have reached completion or production; however, the others all did.

The distinction between a *zarzuela* and an *opereta* is hard to pin down. *Zarzuela*, the older of the two terms, may imply a shorter and slighter piece, although many Spanish-language stage works of full length are called by this name; again, in the early zarzuelas the plot and musical flavour often relate to regional customs, the operettas being more urban and universal. No details about *El Copihue* have been located, beyond the title and zarzuela genre designation. The title refers to the Chilean national flower, often regarded as a symbol of the native cultures—an indigenous reference that may relate this piece to *Rucacahuiñ,* with its emphasis on "aboriginal customs."

Among six or eight professional productions (plays, musicals) on view simultaneously that season in various Santiago theatres, the première of *Rucacahuiñ* on 23 July 1908 reportedly achieved "a success both noisy and well deserved": "It is without doubt the most important work produced in our national theatre in many years…The script is faultless, sharply original, but the score achieves even more: outstanding for its instrumentation, harmony, and expression, this is music, in a word, worthy of an artist…The authors were recalled several times to the stage; however, in the absence of the composer, Señor Alberto García Guerrero, only the librettist was able to appear."[44] Another journalist remarked that the work "gave a good idea of the state of this class of production, so abundant in recent months." At its tenth performance, *Rucacahuiñ* was seen as "unquestionably the greatest success attained up to now by Chilean authors."[45]

The piece is in one act, two scenes. The cast consists of a native chieftain ("cacique araucano"), Puelpán, and eight other native characters, six male ("indios") and two female ("indias"); three "colonos"; and the chieftain's wife, Juana, the adopted orphan daughter of a Spanish officer. The title, as one of the characters explains, is a composite of two Mapuche terms: *ruca,* meaning a hut, and *cahuín* (also spelled *cahuiñ*), meaning a celebration or party. Puelpán is the host of the Rucacahuiñ, and a male chorus sings:

> The Araucanian nation was a land of heroes,
> Of noble chiefs of boldness and courage.
> Their spears triumphed high in the Andes,
> "In fields and valleys and great forests"
> Where the sun's rays never reach.
> Our homeland is no longer what it was,
> The Mapuche nation is no longer free.
> We have lost the fields and valleys
> And only with great effort can we maintain,
> As a miserable nest, this hut.
> No matter, the old Machin commands,
> Let's go contented to the Rucacahuiñ.

Costume designs from the original production of Guerrero's one-act zarzuela *Rucacahuiñ*, from Juan Pablo Gonzalez and Claudio Rolle, *Historia Social de la Música Popular en Chile, 1890–1950* (Santiago: Ediciones Universidad Católica Chile, 2005), by permission.

(The Araucanians are a tribe of the Mapuche, the most numerous of the four indigenous peoples of Chile; Machin refers to a shaman or witch doctor.) One of the "indios," a comic-servant type named Filuñamco, tells the Spanish intruders of Juana's origins: she was kidnapped at age five by natives in a vengeance attack on a Spanish military fort, raised by Puelpán's predecessor as his daughter, and married to Puelpán at the old chief's death. Her beauty, wisdom, and devotion to her husband and his people are central to the story. The plot's climactic event is the acceptance of Filuñamco's Spanish opposite number, Chávez, as an honorary member of the tribe. The *Mundo Teatral* version of the libretto indicates four musical numbers—the chorus excerpted above, an instrumental "intermedio musical" separating the two scenes, a solo for Chávez, and a reprise of this at the final curtain. The opening-night reviewer commends the performer playing Juana for her singing of a romance; that no such number appears in the published libretto raises the possibility it may be a digest rather than the full script.[46]

By coincidence, the Díaz Meza-Guerrero piece has several remarkable features in common with an operetta produced in Canada in roughly the same period, *Le Fétiche* (libretto by Alex Villandray and Louis Fleur, music by Joseph Vézina), first given in Quebec City in February 1912.[47] In both works, characters from native and colonist communities are treated in equal depth; both relate to actual episodes of inter-racial conflict in their countries' histories; and both, moreover, have a more serious dramatic tone than usual in the operetta or comic-opera genre. Though it is unlikely their creators knew of each other's work, both the Chileans and the Canadians show sympathy for the artistic movements of those years aimed at studying and preserving what was considered a disappearing aboriginal way of life.

✦ ✦

17

Damas de Moda, described as an operetta in three acts, is adapted from Victorien Sardou's farce *Divorçons,* first produced in Paris in 1880. A literal translation of Sardou's title—"Let's Get a Divorce"—might have appeared scandalous in 1914 Chile; hence the milder "Ladies of Fashion." According to the script, there were seventeen musical numbers, at least twelve of which had lyrics; the spoken dialogue appears in full, but regrettably the lyrics are not given. The headings indicate five sung duets, a "comic trio," two "romanzas," a sequence of "coplas coreadas" (presumably sung verses with dancing), instrumental dance music, a march, and choral finales to each act. Clearly, the work's musical content was substantial.

The librettos of *Rucacahuiñ* and *Damas de Moda* at least allow us to imagine their form and flavour—something which is not possible with Guerrero's other stage ventures. But sadly, not one of the musical scores of these pieces survives. This is all the more astonishing when one considers the multiplicity of materials—piano-and-voice scores, full scores, orchestral parts—required in mounting such works. (With that in mind, however, it is possible to hope that with further searching some fragments may yet emerge.) It becomes especially frustrating in these circumstances to read a reviewer's comments on particular niceties of the music. A further frustration is that no documentation has so far come to light of the evidently close working relationship between Guerrero and Díaz Meza. In contrast to his virtuoso concertizing, already outlined, and his devotion to intimate reformist or avant-garde movements such as the Cañas-Besaoín circle, the Academia Ortiz de Zárate, Los Diez, and the embryonic Sociedad Bach, to be described shortly, here we may at least glimpse the young Guerrero at the same time also in touch with the world of popular stage comedy.

Two Composer-Associates

Closely associated with Guerrero in his early career were two contemporaries, both of whom became outstanding figures in composition, education, and the reform of Chilean musical life. Alfonso Leng Haygus (1884–1974), cellist and composer from a partly German background, pursued a second professional career as an odontologist and became internationally known also in that field. Domingo Santa Cruz Wilson (1899–1987) qualified as a lawyer and for a time served in the Chilean diplomatic service, besides his musical prominence as composer and as founder of the Faculty of Fine Arts of the Universidad de Chile in the late 1920s. (A square adjacent to the faculty building in Santiago now bears his name.)

Leng and Guerrero were fellow students of music: both were largely self-taught, according to the main biographical sources, though Leng evidently had some composition lessons from 1905 to 1906 with Enrique Soro at the Conservatorio. In 1911 Guerrero published a brief appreciation of Leng's work in the journal *Negro y blanco*.[48] As already noted, he played piano and Leng cello in a trio with the violinist Humberto Busenius in concerts in 1912, and he and his brother Eduardo both played active roles in the Academia Ortiz de Zárate founded by Leng that year. An archive of the long-running series of musicales held in the homes of Luis Arrieta Cañas and José Miguel Besoaín records Guerrero's frequent participation—for example, seven performances of Debussy's *L'isle joyeuse* and three of the same composer's *En bâteau* in the years 1911, '12, and '13. Leng attended many of these sessions, as did other composers such as Cotapos, Soro, and Humberto Allende.[49] They seem to have had a didactic purpose, combining performance and explication. (The particular Debussy works offered for discussion are an interesting and unexpected pair—*L'isle joyeuse* (1905) being one of the most mature and highly developed of his piano compositions, and *En bâteau* (1889) a slighter early work, arranged from his four-hand *Petite suite*.)

Earlier, Leng had pursued professional studies in the school of dentistry and is supposed to have persuaded his younger colleague to do the same. Guerrero is said by various chroniclers to have attended the dental program for a year, or for two or even three years, before abandoning this potential career in favour of a musical one.[50] His motivation, besides the urging of Leng, may have been family pressure: professional certification (though not yet a degree: the dental college did not affiliate with the university until later) was considered a desirable asset in a young person of his class, however artistically gifted. But the Faculty of Dentistry has no record in its archives of his ever having registered for the program.[51] At most he may have attended classes for a few weeks without making a formal registration, but even for this there is no documentary evidence.

Leng's birth date is wrongly given as 1894 (instead of 1884) in a number of leading reference works, which may be the source of the notion that he was Guerrero's student; it appears more accurate to say they engaged in mutual studies of music. On several occasions in later years, Leng described Guerrero's intellectual influence on his own work and that of other contemporaries in Chile. Such influence, a matter of guidance and advice rather than formal study, was nonetheless formidable: "all the composers of his time—Lavín, Cotapos, Bisquertt, Leng, and, some years afterwards, Domingo Santa Cruz—submitted their compositions to Alberto García Guerrero's judgment and the two last-named have acknowledged his influence."[52]

The emergence of Guerrero as a youthful guru, among the musical live wires of his time, may be sensed from the historical summary of the period by Eugenio Pereira Salas:

Chile was slow to adapt to this tumultuous uncharted world [of music, 1912–17]....Deserving special mention is the trio of the García Guerrero brothers. In the library of Alberto, the pianist and composer, the treatises of Rieman [sic] and D'Indy sat alongside scores of Debussy, Ravel, and Schoenberg, which he performed in private readings with widespread effect. Carlos Lavín's research in French music periodicals provoked much discussion....The "Los Diez" group created a fraternal synthesis of poetry, art, and music. The Biblioteca Nacional sponsored lectures concerning the biographies of the great masters. Pedro Humberto Allende explored contemporary orchestral techniques. Juan Casanova Vicuña undertook concert performances of symphonic works by Debussy and Ravel.[53]

The Academia Ortiz de Zárate was named for the composer of *La florista di Lugano,* Eliodoro Ortiz de Zárate (1865–1953). The Academia was "an organization founded by a young group, among them Eduardo García Guerrero, who became its president, the violinist Humberto Busenius, and the cellists Alfonso Leng and Valenzuela Llanos."[54] Guerrero's brother Eduardo, mainly known as a writer and a critic of both politics and music, was responsible for getting together an informal orchestra within the Academia's membership: "this orchestra, meeting irregularly, showed Eduardo García as a natural musician, who directed the players with deep intuition more than from technical mastery."[55] The Academia is described as the continuation of a series of musical gatherings previously held in the García Guerreros' home; other members included Alberto Guerrero and the composer Carlos Lavín (1883–1962), their aim being to explore the works of European composers of the new century.[56]

In 1914, when the artistic circle Los Diez gathered, with the writer Pedro Prado as "spiritual father," the musical members were Guerrero, Leng, and their younger colleague Acario Cotapos, a composer later active in the USA and in France.

This group, referred to in one historical survey as "Chilean culture's first centre of avant-gardism," espoused modern movements in writing, painting, music, and architecture.[57] Though dubbed the Group of Ten, its members, affiliates, and sympathizers eventually numbered more than ten. It began when the architect Julio Bertrand challenged Prado's claim that it would not be difficult to find ten similar-minded young artists in Chile. At early informal gatherings the participants included these two as well as the poets Armando Donoso and Manuel Magallanes Moure, the sculptor Alberto Ried, and the painters Julio Ortiz de Zárate (son of the composer) and Juan Francisco González (an older figure). An art exhibition in 1914 brought the group its first public attention; several of the literary members also offered paintings and drawings. A significant organ of mutual propagandizing was

Cover, special issue of the journal *Los Diez* 1, no. 9 (May 1917) (Biblioteca Nacional, Santiago)

the journal *Los Diez,* of which ten issues were produced in 1916–17; both Eduardo and Alberto García Guerrero were contributors—Eduardo as critical writer and Alberto as composer. Though acting cohesively for only a few seasons, the group is credited with wide influence in Chilean cultural history. A lasting monument in the country's musical repertoire is *La muerte de Alsino,* 1922, an orchestral tone-poem by Leng based on the novel of the same name by Prado.[58]

A commentator on Cotapos's early musical formation singles out the "important work" of Guerrero and Lavín in "renovating the musical vocabulary of the Chilean public...in the first two decades of the century"—an indication that, like Leng and Santa Cruz, Cotapos also recognized Guerrero's collegial influence.[59]

Domingo Santa Cruz, by his own later account, did study music with Guerrero, and always acknowledged the latter's encouragement and guidance during his teen years when he was preparing for a musical vocation.[60] Santa Cruz was a cousin of Lily Wilson, Guerrero's first wife: her father and his mother were brother and sister. He paints a vivid picture of his early contacts with Guerrero: a fellow student, Carlos Humeres, he says, "revealed to me the greatness of Bach's works, which in general were hardly regarded by people at that time as much different from ordinary piano exercises. Carlos Humeres's sisters were excellent pianists, and, thanks to the influence of Alberto García Guerrero, it was at their home that I first became acquainted with contemporary music in works by Debussy and Ravel."[61] Santa Cruz's own siblings were all musical, and in his family circle "there was a great love of Italian opera, the centre of musical activity in those days." But he found this enthusiasm vulgar, and preferred to read Beethoven symphonies in four-handed piano arrangements with Humeres.

> I was indebted to Carlos for putting me in contact with García Guerrero, the man whose cultural influence one encounters at the root of all musical initiatives. Alberto García Guerrero looked at my first compositions, encouraged me, gave me advice, and proposed to teach me the piano. I soon convinced him of the futility of his patience as a teacher....We then resolved that the lessons would consist of score reading and conversation [about music]. He urged me to read the *Revista S.I.M.* from Paris and analyzed for me the quartets of Schoenberg and the technique of that composer. Through him I came to know the music of Debussy, which he played marvellously and of which he had profound knowledge. [He] introduced me to Alfonso Leng and we became great friends. Leng sang in the Sociedad Bach choir, and never missed one of our sessions.[62]

It was in the salons of various cultivated Santiago families—among them the Humeres and Canales families—that the Sociedad Bach gradually emerged; the first meetings took place in June 1917.[63] We are told that Guerrero and his brother Eduardo participated.[64] At first a series of readings, by an amateur choir, of music by Palestrina, J.S. Bach, Beethoven, and Mendelssohn, the society's programs broadened within a few months to include major works of European instrumental music that had been previously neglected by Chilean musicians, and therefore little appreciated by the musical public. Naming the collective after Bach seems to have been the inspiration of the choirmaster at the cathedral, Father Vicente Carrasco, a fanatic Bach devotee who was known to carry the score of the *St. Matthew Passion* next to his breviary.[65] Along with the pioneering amateur-orchestra ventures of the Academia, the efforts of the Sociedad brought increased enlightenment and sophistication to the country's musical scene.

Cultural historians credit these various initiatives—seen, at least in part, as emanations of Guerrero's influence—with creating a climate for the eventual establishment of a higher level of musical performance and education, and of musical taste generally, in Chile in the late 1920s and 1930s. Claudio Arrau returned to Santiago to play his first complete cycle of J.S. Bach's *Well-Tempered Clavier* in 1924, sponsored by the Sociedad Bach. One of the further contributions of Santa Cruz as first dean of the

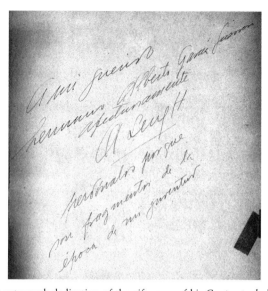

Alfonso Leng's autograph dedication of the gift score of his *Cuatro preludios para piano*, 1929 (Faculty of Music library, University of Toronto)

fine arts faculty at the Universidad de Chile was the inauguration of the scholarly periodical *Revista musical chilena*, which was still flourishing in 2004.

A copy of *Cuatro preludios para piano*, a short published work by Leng, was inscribed by the composer as follows: "To my dear brother Alberto García Guerrero, affectionately, A. Leng H.—[with] apologies that these are fragments from the period of my youth."[66] Leng and Santa Cruz both made periodic tours to North America for professional meetings and performances, and apparently visited Guerrero in Toronto during their travels. Leng records, in a short memoir, that he was in the audience for Glenn Gould's 1947 performance of Beethoven's Concerto no. 4 with the Toronto Symphony Orchestra; Gould, then fourteen, impressed him as a gifted young inheritor of Guerrero's approach to performance.[67] A note from Leng's widow, María Eugenia Cuevas Mackenna, and sister-in-law, Carmen Cuevas Mackenna, recalls Leng's visit with Guerrero in Toronto at that time. Leng apparently reported his reception as friendly but cool: he was surprised that Guerrero showed little interest or curiosity about events in his native country.[68] At one of my lessons in the late 1940s, I remember, Guerrero placed on the music rack a new piano piece he had just received by post from Leng (not the *Cuatro preludios*), and asked me to sight-read it.

Writings

The researcher of Guerrero's early musical activities, dismayed at the lost concert programs and the lost or destroyed compositions, may be further crushed at the disappearance of critical and analytical writings he is known to have published.

Of his concert and opera reviews and longer critical pieces in *El Diario ilustrado,* Santiago, between 1905 and 1910, some are signed "A.G.G." or "A.G." while many others, quite possibly by him, were published with no signature. That the newspaper was founded in 1902 means he was engaged (at age nineteen!) in only its third year of operation. His characterization as a professional music critic is in some accounts inflated, perhaps in confusion with his brother Eduardo's later position in that capacity with *El Mercurio.* That journal's coverage of musical life was intermittent and anonymous in the early 1910s, but became more regular from mid-1915, when the byline "Valsy" (likely Eduardo's pseudonym) appears at least weekly. The extent of Eduardo's activity as a critic exceeded that of his young brother.

But Alberto hardly lacked for either literary flair or sharp opinions, judging from a selection of his reviews. The *Diario* editors appear to have valued the work of their youthful music correspondent: on several occasions they gave his reviews a featured position on the paper's front page. A series of three reviews in 1907 covers a cycle of chamber-music recitals at the Teatro de Variedades by the Trio Giarda. Despite the name, the company, headed by the cellist Luigi Stephano Giarda, presented works in a number of different ensemble formations.[69] Guerrero's notices are significant for two reasons: one, they illustrate his growing acquaintance with music literature, and especially with newly composed pieces (he describes at length works by Dvořák, Rubinstein, and Richard Strauss); and two, they show him speaking out in favour of expanded and elevated musical tastes with the Chilean public of his day. For example:

> This sympathetic artistic group, the only one in existence today here in Santiago with the laudable aim of cultivating acquaintance with the chamber works of the great masters, deserves all the plaudits which have been aroused by its efforts and the ever-increasing success of its enterprise…. Here, where performers of some real merit disappear in obscurity, the efforts of the Variedades concerts are worthy of the highest praise as they raise the artistic level of our public, formerly satisfied with the *Toscas* and *Fedoras* of the opera companies, affording them a knowledge of the works of the great composers.[70]

Such opinions were, as noted already, frequently voiced in the ensuing years by young artists of Guerrero's generation in Chile, and the great instrumental repertoire of eighteenth- and nineteenth-century Europe was increasingly stressed over the consuming general-public passion for Italian opera. But opera was also part of Guerrero's critical purview. In a pair of "think-pieces" in 1907 he evaluated the soloists and surveyed the artistic policies of the Teatro Municipal's opera season. The writing exudes authority and high standards—indeed, the tone is one of youthful bravado. He claims, "It is easy to find artists who can interpret Puccini with feeling...or put across Leoncavallo and Mascagni in tender fashion and pleasingly for an audience; however, to undertake a great work of art, as Señora [Virginia] Guerrini does in *Samson and Delilah,* is to appreciate the difference between Saint-Saens and [Leoncavallo]." In reviewing the company's current baritones ("¡Oh, los baritonos!"), he recalls, from earlier productions, De Luca's Scarpia, Paccini's Rigoletto, and Nani's Count de Luna, to emphasize the decline. On the other hand, Livia Berlendi's "rare, fine, penetrating, and subtle temperament allows her to reveal the most deeply hidden details of her roles, and with her sharp psychological intuition (a trendy sort of psychology, granted) she gives us portrayals like Massenet's Manon that are admirable in their intelligence and well-assimilated style." The repertoire overview mentions eleven titles of current productions, with various favourable and unfavourable comments—the company's tenors take a beating, but Berlendi's Tosca and, especially, Guerrini's Amneris stand out—and he longs for the day when the company can undertake a *Tannhäuser* or a *Lohengrin.*[71] Reviews of individual operas, including Puccini's *Manon Lescaut* and *Madama Butterfly* and Catalani's *Loreley,* though unsigned, suggest Guerrero's voice.[72] The *Butterfly* is judged to have been well performed; however, "We can only regret that the company chose for its opening night an opera which properly belongs in the operetta theatre."

In a thoughtful essay on Ambroise Thomas's *Hamlet,* this time signed with his initials, Guerrero refers to the critical comments of the French writer [Louis] Étienne Destranges, characterizing the work of Thomas as

> a mixture of various dissimilar styles—those most in vogue in his day— the main ones being the clever traces of good humour of his teacher, Auber; the general tendencies of the French school in sticking to tradition; and one or other of the noisiest late arrivals from Germany.

> It is not hard to discern in *Hamlet* [Thomas's] desire to please everyone and shock no one, which in the end removes all unity from the work and leaves only a heterogeneous mix where fine ideas and sincere expressions, intended for a cultivated audience, parade alongside countless concessions to the gross public. After the first-act duet of Hamlet and Ophelia, for example, with its phrases of lovely delicacy such as that marking

Ophelia's entrance, comes a chorus of court officials of the most vulgar effect.

These alternations occur in every scene of Thomas's opera, reaching an almost-ultimate point of triviality in the fourth act, where except for the "ballade" of Ophelia there is nothing but a series of polkas, waltzes, and mazurkas of the cheapest kind...

The libretto is written along the same artistic lines as the music....Such is the adaptation of Barbier and Carré that Hamlet becomes a boor, retaining nothing of the complicated and powerful individuality depicted by Shakespeare.

The baritone Giraldoni, who appeared in Santiago in the title role, had received enthusiastic applause and critiques. But the young A.G.G. begged to differ: "Without wishing to dispute these appreciations, we observed the celebrated baritone slithering onto the stage, making a thousand contortions and gestures, fighting desperately to detach himself from opponents who seemed not to be exerting the slightest effort to attack him, and eventually bringing to our mind the advice of Hamlet to the players in Shakespeare's drama: 'Nor do not saw the air too much with your hand.'"[73]

From journalistic assignments, Guerrero appears to have gone on to more scholarly writing projects. Chilean sources all mention his treatise *La armonía moderna,* published in Santiago in 1915. For example, Alfonso Leng claims that "[Guerrero's] profound knowledge of harmony, counterpoint, and fugue, and his original concepts concerning these disciplines, led him to write a treatise on harmony, which, by its marvellous pedagogical insights, is a work of extraordinary importance, since it deals with the most complex of today's harmonic systems."[74] Searches for this publication in music libraries, with rare-book dealers, and even in Leng's own family archives, have so far failed to locate a copy.

A second treatise from around the same date by Guerrero, this one articulating his ideas on piano performance, has similarly disappeared, although whether it ever advanced from the preparation stage to actual publication is not verified. Guerrero spoke about it with Emilio Uzcátegui García a short while before leaving Santiago in 1918:

He is at present preparing a manual on piano technique and no doubt its reception will be completely favourable, given the author's important work of research and the modern concepts it will put forward concerning the study of this instrument. [About this work Guerrero says:] "In general, in piano as in voice and in all musical instruments, the move is towards a more logical and natural use of all the individual performer's faculties. In piano, this leads us to discard all formal methods of teaching. These days each artist ought to be directed by special (individual) studies."

"Now we understand the secret of the grand technicians such as Liszt and Rubinstein, which so stunned the European public." "The main result of this acquisition to which the scientific study of the piano has led, is this: a person of average gifts may attain, in a much shorter time than previously, the technique which formerly was only afforded by a few. Given the view which we now have of what piano instruction should be, I can claim that a reasonably well gifted person needs no more than four or five years of well-directed study to be able to handle the technical demands of the most difficult works."[75]

two

A Wedding, a Tour

Guerrero's most active season as a performer, 1915, was also the time of his marriage. His bride, Elena ("Lily") Wilson, was the oldest daughter of a distinguished military figure, Lieutenant Colonel Aníbal Wilson Navarrete, and his wife María Werner Araya, and niece of an equally prominent leader in the Chilean Navy, Admiral Arturo Wilson Navarrete.[1] The family was well recognized from the brothers' careers in the forces, and also for its cultivation of literature and the arts. In the late months of 1915, Guerrero and his cellist colleague Michael Penha undertook a successful tour, playing joint concerts in the main cities of Peru, Bolivia, Panama, Costa Rica, and Cuba, before settling in New York—and Lily was a member of the touring party; indeed, the tour was referred to in family circles later as the couple's honeymoon. A reporter in Oruro, Bolivia, noted during one of the concerts "the presentation of a bouquet of wild flowers to Señora Wilson de García Guerrero, by which members of the Chilean community wanted to express their feelings of respect for this distinguished lady." In Lima, Peru, a concert notice included the information that "Señor García Guerrero, a member of the Santiago aristocracy (*la aristocracia santiaguina*), is accompanied by his wife, the distinguished Señora Lilli [*sic*] Wilson de García Guerrero, niece of the noted Chilean admiral of the same name."[2]

Possibly as a fundraiser for their tour, Guerrero and Penha gave a widely publicized farewell concert in the Teatro Septiembre, Santiago, on 14 September 1915. Penha, born and educated in Holland, had by that time been in Chile a little over a year and a half, and is said to have made an

Lily Wilson, at the time of her marriage to Alberto Guerrero, 1915 (Collection M. Irvine)

indelible impression in a succession of concerts covering much of the standard classical repertoire for cello. Referring to his "fiery temperament," "nobility of interpretation," and "impeccable virtuosity," Alfonso Leng called him "one of the greatest executants to have visited here."[3] In another advance article for this concert, the writer, Carlos Silva Cruz, appears less familiar with Penha's work, but wishes the two artists a "glorious triumph," despite the feelings of sadness at their departure. Of Guerrero, Silva Cruz writes more spontaneously, mentioning his "profound interpretations of the major works for piano, as evidenced in his own solo concerts, his performances with Penha, and the illustrations he played for those lovely lectures of his brother Eduardo. He has always enjoyed the warmest rapport with the public—a rapport only won by the truest and most cultivated talents."[4]

The concert was on an unusually grand scale. An orchestra led by Luigi Giarda played an unspecified overture by Mendelssohn, and then each of the artists was featured in a concerto: Penha in a Saint-Saens cello concerto (perhaps no. 2 in d), and Guerrero in the same composer's Fourth Piano Concerto. The program concluded with solo groups. Here Penha presented an arrangement for cello and piano of Dvořák's *Silent Woods*, Opus 68, no. 5, followed by David Popper's Tarantella, while Guerrero's solo numbers were two pieces by Liszt he had frequently included in earlier programs: *Liebestraum* and the Hungarian Rhapsody no. 11.

Leng's tribute to Guerrero, in his advance article, summed up the position he was seen to hold in Chilean musical life at this period:

> Of our compatriot, the distinguished pianist Alberto García Guerrero, we can say little that is not already known by every aficionado who has followed with interest the steps of his artistic career. As a pianist…he has advanced to the forefront among our performers, not only by his exceptional gifts of temperament but also by his understanding of the styles of all the great masters. But there is also a facet of his talent that is not well known among us, and this is his personal voice as a composer. Those who know the serious works of García Guerrero…recognize in them a profound technical mastery of composition and an originality which evokes the subtlest feelings and the most elevated emotions.[5]

As a friend and fellow composer, Leng may have felt a special need to stress, in drawing public attention to the event, this other side of Guerrero's achievement.

The two colleagues, Penha and Guerrero, were launched on their ambitious tour with the praise and good wishes of the Santiago audience to carry them confidently along. In the ensuing three-and-a-half months they gave joint concerts in La Paz and Oruro, Bolivia; Arequipa and Lima, Peru; Panama City, Panama; San José, Costa Rica; and Havana, Cuba. In several centres they evidently played not just one but two or even three concerts. The tour may have included other stops, for which records are lacking.

A concert on 2 October in the Biógrafo París, La Paz, sponsored by the Círculo de Bellas Artes, evidently the opening concert of the tour, offered the following program:

1. Grieg: Sonata Opus 36 for cello and piano
2. (piano) Chopin: Nocturne; Waltz; Ballade no. 3 in A flat, Opus 47
3. (cello) Maurage: *Song of the Swan;* Davidov: *At the Fountain*
4. (piano) Liszt: *Liebestraum;* Hungarian Rhapsody no. 11
5. (cello) Schumann: *Abendlied;* Sinding: *Ritornello;* Valensin: Minuet; Jeral: *Slavic Dance*

This program was repeated in other centres, sometimes opening with a different duo-sonata in place of the Grieg. A second concert in the same hall seems to have been followed by a third, in the Teatro Municipal on 16 October, with the following program:

1. Bréval: Sonata for cello and piano
2. (piano) Chopin: Fantaisie-impromptu; Wagner arr. Liszt: *Isolde's Liebestod;* Ravel: *Jeux d'eau*
3. (cello) Schumann: *Rêverie*[6]; Fischer: *Czardas*

4. (piano) Chaminade: *Automne;* Schubert arr. Liszt: Lied [probably *Hark, hark, the lark*]; Chopin: Étude Opus 10, no. 3 and Waltz Opus 69, no. 1; Mendelssohn: Scherzo
5. (cello) Boldi: *Romanza bohemia;* Van Goens: Scherzo; Saint-Saens: *The Swan;* Popper: Tarantella

To the items on these two programs, there were occasional additions; for example, Léon Boëllmann's *Symphonic Variations,* Opus 23, for cello and piano, several times. A review in San José, Costa Rica, mentions other titles not found in the printed programs which have been preserved— (cello) Huré's Aria, Pierné's Serenade, Grainger's *Swedish Melody,* and (piano) Chopin's Barcarolle and Études Opus 25, nos. 1 and 9; Liszt's Concert Étude [probably *La leggierrezza*] and Polonaise; and Sgambati's Minuet. The Costa Rica program appears to have been the only one that included an original work by Guerrero—his *Capricho* for piano, given as an encore. The programs appear designed to highlight the performers first in a classical-chamber-music format and then in works of virtuosic and expressive content from their respective repertoires. For Guerrero this meant generous helpings of Chopin and Liszt, current concert favourites by Giovanni Sgambati, Cécile Chaminade, or Benjamin Godard, and a few up-to-the-minute items by Debussy or Ravel or both. For Penha it meant music by cellist-composers from the eighteenth century (Jean-Baptiste Bréval, Johann Wenzel von Sporck) and the nineteenth (Hugo Becker, Karl Davidov, Julius Klengel, David Popper).

The enthusiasm engendered by their appearances is a measure of the isolation felt in some of even the larger towns visited, with their limited exposure to professional artistic efforts. For example, for the concert of 26 October in Arequipa, Peru, a flyer promised a "Grand Concert by the notable artistic team García Guerrero–Penha, comprising the eminent recitalists Alberto García Guerrero, pianist, and Michael Penha, cellist, now on a tour of the American republics: only appearance in Arequipa." The event constitutes, we're breathlessly told, "the first time our distinguished public has the chance to hear two artists of the calibre of our visitors—an opportunity which only rarely presents itself, to welcome an artistic team which has been so enthusiastically applauded in the major South American centres." The newspaper in Oruro, Bolivia, picturesquely described the performers as "birds of passage, who have come to our town here in the highest reaches of the Andes, to impress us with their beautiful and generous art." The reviews used terms like "veritable triumph," and "complete success." In San José, Costa Rica, a critic ventured to call their concert "the most brilliant [artistic success] ever recorded in the cultural annals of the country."

Indeed, it was at the concert of 21 December in San José that the reaction of the audience was most animated: "Following the notable musical presentation given in the Teatro Nacional by the renowned artists Michael Penha and Alberto García Guerrero, their enthusiastic public accompanied these gentlemen to their lodgings in the Hotel Francis, cheering them through the streets. Everywhere in the capital there is favourable talk of the resounding triumph gained by these performers last night." The recitals attracted large audiences throughout the tour, an exception being the concert of 5 December at the National Conservatory in Panama City, attended by "a small audience of Americans and Panamanians." The event, however, received the usual applause and critical bravos.

An advance article for the concert of 16 January 1916 in Havana alleges that Penha and Guerrero had collaborated on previous tours to other parts of South America:

> From the notices of both artists we are aware that, with a brilliant series of concerts in the cosmopolitan centre of Buenos Aires, they have embarked on a tour of the principal cities, their eventual goal being the republic to the North. We know of these famous artists by what has been said of them in the press in Argentina, Uruguay, Chile, Bolivia, and elsewhere. From reviews in every country they have reaped the warmest acclamations. We hope their stay in Havana will be a significant marker in their triumphant progress.

The information about prior appearances and touring, found here but so far nowhere else, is hard to confirm, and may apply to Penha alone, rather than to his partnership with Guerrero.

The tour covered a large territory, and the generous welcoming notices suggest that in many places it made a distinct and memorable contribution to local musical life. Penha and Guerrero continued to collaborate after settling in the USA, playing together both in New York and in other centres. The two seem to have become firm friends as well as sympathetic artistic colleagues. After Guerrero's departure for Toronto, Penha was for five years first cellist of the Philadelphia Orchestra. He then settled in Los Angeles, where he played in the orchestra of one of the large motion-picture studios. In 1949 he was cellist in the California premiere of Messiaen's *Quartet for the End of Time* for the "Evenings on the Roof" concert series.

Ray Dudley met Penha in California in the middle 1950s and they talked about Guerrero. The suggestion that in his youth Guerrero had been headed for the priesthood came from Penha; he claimed this was automatic in Chilean families as a role for the youngest son. Speaking of the New York years, Penha told Dudley he recalled having seen Guerrero and his wife off on the boat to South America in 1917. With war looming, musical life in New York was not favourable, and many professional opportunities had been suspended. Penha further recalled that he was with Guerrero in New York when they happened to meet the pianist Mark Hambourg on the street and Hambourg told Guerrero of a position available at the then-new Hambourg Conservatory in Toronto.[7] The exact date of this chance meeting, the overture to Guerrero's Canadian career, is unknown. It likely took place before the Guerreros' late-1917 departure. A caricature of Michael Penha appears on the cover of the October 1917 issue of the *Canadian Journal of Music*, a Toronto publication.[8] Inside the issue there is a short promotional article about him containing, however, no mention of any pending engagement in Toronto. It is not known whether in fact he ever made a professional appearance in Canada.

Information concerning Guerrero's possible later collaborations with Penha—that is, after New York—is a matter of a few hints only. In a letter of 1951, Guerrero refers to "a friend" with whom he had visited Paris in 1925, recalling also other meetings in Holland and Cuba, without dates.[9] This unnamed acquaintance or colleague was no doubt Michael Penha. Guerrero's European tours or visits before the mid-1930s are largely a matter of hearsay and conjecture; there is no further documentation; but this passage from his letter suggests there were further concert activities there with Penha.

Caricature of the cellist Michael Penha, artist unknown (*Canadian Journal of Music* 4, no. 6 [October 1917])

New York and Back: A Farewell

The final stop on the tour was New York, and the Guerreros appear to have established their home there for about a year and a half. The New York city directory for 1917 gives their address as 345 West 191 Street, at the far northern tip of Manhattan Island, near Fort Tyron Park, not far from the present Cloisters.

A printed brochure, in English, produced in 1916 or '17, offers concerts by the team of Penha and Guerrero. After their successful and groundbreaking tour, engagements were sparse. A concert for an unidentified "Pickwick Club" on 6 March 1916 alternated solo groups for piano and for cello, with no major duo pieces. A pair of concerts in New Orleans, 18 and 22 March, repeated the sort of joint programs that had been featured on the tour. Promotional notices had an ethnic slant, speaking of "Señor Penha, who, in spite of his Portuguese name, was born in Holland," and referring to Guerrero as "one of the most eminent composers of the far South," adding that "Their appearance should be of special interest to the rapidly increasing Spanish population of New Orleans."[10] Held in Gibson Hall, Tulane University, the concerts brought complimentary reviews in the national music press as well as locally.

There may have been a concert in Chicago at this period: it is virtually certain that Guerrero visited Chicago and saw Mary Garden in Debussy's *Pelléas et Mélisande,* and a concert engagement could well have coincided, though no program has been preserved. There were no mountings of this opera in New York during Guerrero's brief time of residence (the Manhattan Opera Company had performed it in the early 1910s, but it was not done at the Metropolitan Opera until 1923). It was of course the deeply impressive experience of *Pelléas* which prompted Alberto and Lily to name their child Mélisande.

Concert appearances before the New York public had to wait until the fall season of 1916. A notice in the *Musical Courier* records a concert at the Aeolian Hall by Penha and Guerrero, on 12 October of that year.[11] The program included Guerrero's *Chants oubliés*—"a very modern piece of writing"—in what may have been its first performance.

Another Aeolian Hall concert, on 14 December, was shared with Rudolf Ruckert, described as "a German-Italian basso," and his piano accompanist Willy Tyroler, "a German conductor of the Metropolitan Opera House."[12] The same report identified Guerrero as "a South American composer-pianist, who made his New York début [on this occasion]," ignoring his prior appearances in the city. The program contents are not known in full. After criticizing the singer and the cellist for uncertainties in intonation, A.H. in *Musical America* went on:

Alberto García Guerrero, the cellist's accompanist, was the artistic hero of the recital. He played the accompaniments excellently and performed two of his own compositions, "Chants oubliés" and a Danse. The works were so Ornsteinly original that the audience at first thought that the pianist was emulating the pitch-free example of Mr. Ruckert and Mr. Penha. We will probably hear more from this young Mr. Guerrero.[13]

The smartness of this review—its superior frown at technical discrepancies, its reference to the then-current ne plus ultra of modernity, Leo Ornstein, and its assured mind reading of the audience—strikes an altogether different tone from the adulatory critiques that had met Guerrero and Penha on their tour. If they had expected to conquer New York, New York was being tough about it. It is unclear, though this event was called his "début," whether either it or the previous one in October included any piano solos by Guerrero; the two compositions mentioned are duos.

Page from Guerrero's *Chants oubliés* for cello and piano, New York, 1916, in the composer's autograph score (Guerrero Collection). Fingering of the cello line probably by Michael Penha; the signature of six flats, appearing only on the first page, is implied throughout.

The Passaic, New Jersey, *Daily Herald* of 5 December 1916 notes briefly a recital in which Guerrero participated, whether as soloist or accompanist or both is uncertain because the program is missing. No date is given for this event. A program is, however, preserved for a joint concert by Guerrero with the violinist Abram Haitovich, in Witherspoon Hall, Philadelphia, on 20 January 1917. Haitovich played Mendelssohn's Concerto in e, Opus 64, Saint-Saens's *Rondo capriccioso*, Sarasate's *Zigeunerweisen,* and a solo group of shorter numbers, while Guerrero was heard in two solo groups, the first made up of Debussy's *Jardins sous la pluie* and *Pagodes* and Ravel's *Jeux d'eau,* and the second two works by Chopin: a Waltz (evidently Opus 70, no. 1 in G flat) and the Scherzo no. 3 in c sharp, Opus 39. The *Philadelphia Inquirer*'s reviewer found them "delightfully played."

The following 14 April, Guerrero was a featured performer at an unusual event—a concert and ball sponsored by the Peretz Writers' Association, with Emilia Gresser, violinist, and Corina Post, soprano, at the Central Opera House, on 67 Street and Third Avenue. The concert started at 8:00 in the evening, to be followed by the ball, from eleven until four the next morning. Guerrero is described on the Yiddish-language poster (in the private collection of Mélisande Irvine) as "the famous composer-pianist"; whether any of his own compositions were featured is not known.[14]

It seems likely there were other performances by Guerrero in the United States during this period, but so far these events are the only ones for which documentation is available.

Guerrero's main work in New York was as studio accompanist to Paul Althouse, the Metropolitan Opera's leading Wagnerian tenor, who was also a prominent and successful voice teacher and coach. Guerrero referred to this connection in later years as a principal source for his knowledge of the Wagner operas.[15] As well, he evidently regularly accompanied Althouse's pupils in their recitals. This activity represented a departure from the almost exclusively instrumental ensemble work that had occupied him during his Chilean years, and it deepened his knowledge of the solo literature for voice.

To this period belongs Guerrero's only surviving vocal composition, the song *To Maud Allan.* He evidently encountered the text, a short poem by the American poet Witter Bynner, in the *Musical Courier.*[16] It does not appear in any of Bynner's published collections. The main imagery is taken from the landscape of northern New Mexico, where Bynner spent most of his adult life. Though unfamiliar with such desert scenes, Guerrero obviously responded to the theme of dedication to beauty:

Poster, concert, and ball, New York, 14 April 1917 (Collection M. Irvine, photo André Leduc)

Cactus of pain and sand
Of barrenness!
Yet even here shall stand
Beauty and bless
With her unfailing hand
And keep me brave
Under the desert sky
And guide and save
Till even I
Shall walk with her untroubled on the grave.

Was this song performed publicly during Guerrero's New York stay, perhaps by a singer from Althouse's studio? Although there is no concrete evidence, it seems likely.

His Santiago composer-colleague and fellow member of Los Diez, Acario Cotapos, was also a resident of New York at this time, and Guerrero's later fond references to him are recalled by Ms. Irvine, suggesting that they were in friendly contact in this new environment.

The New York interlude is the least substantiated part of Guerrero's story. Further research, particularly in newspaper reviews, may enlarge our knowledge of his sojourn, which extended over approximately twenty months. Whereas in Chile he had become a distinguished authority figure, both for fellow professionals and for the musical public, in New York he was one of many struggling young musicians, whose promise lay in the future ("we will probably hear more from this young Mr Guerrero").

In 1917 Lily became pregnant, and they decided to return to Chile for the birth. The child was born in Santiago on 5 November 1917 at seven in the evening, and given her mother's name, Lily (she acquired the name Mélisande only slightly later). Guerrero signed the birth certificate and listed her parents' address vaguely as "*anterior*" ("former residents")—an indication, perhaps, that he did not anticipate resuming Chilean residence.

But before the start of the new year, 1918, he plunged into concert activities, responding to opportunities such as New York had not afforded him. One exceptional engagement took him to Punta Arenas, the most southerly town in Patagonia, more than 2,000 kilometres south of Santiago, in what was apparently his only visit to that part of Chile. Press notices confirm that Guerrero in fact spent nearly a full month there, arriving on the steamer *Magallanes* around 23 December 1917 and departing on the *Avilés* on approximately 22 January 1918. "It is to be hoped that our public, so starved for artistic events, will greet Señor García Guerrero's present visit with pleasure and enthusiasm."[17] The publicist's hopes appear to have been generously fulfilled: on 12 January Guerrero was tendered a testimonial banquet in Punta Arenas by "sus amigos y admiradores." The jokey menu ("Liszt de viandas") fancifully links well-known composers' names with the various courses—"Chopin mayonnaise," "Beethoven soup," and so on; the promised dessert is a "Macedonía de frutas à la García Guerrero." A copy survives with autographs of various attendees: the name "Armando Carvajal" is among the few that are decipherable, which may indicate that Carvajal also took part in this concert visit.[18]

The programs of his three Punta Arenas concerts are remarkable, and suggest that during his New York sojourn he had been conscientiously broadening his performing repertoire:

6 January:
>   Beethoven: Sonata in E flat, Opus 31, no. 3
>   Chopin: Scherzo no.1 in b; Waltz; Ballade no. 3 in A flat; Polonaise
>   Rachmaninov: Prelude in G
>   Liszt: Concert Étude [no. 2]; *Rigoletto Fantasy*

10 January:
>   Schumann: *Études symphoniques*
>   Gluck arr. Brahms: Gavotte; Daquin: *Le Coucou;* Sgambati: Minuet;
>   Beethoven: Écossaises; Chopin: Three Études

Ravel: *Jeux d'eau*; Rachmaninov: Prelude in c sharp; Schubert arr.
Liszt: *Serenade*; Liszt: *La campanella*

13 January:
Bach arr. Liszt: Prelude and Fugue
Wagner arr. Liszt: *Isolde's Love-Death;* Brahms: Capriccio [in b, Opus 76,
no. 2]; Guerrero: *Valse triste;* Debussy: *Jardins sous la pluie;* Chopin:
Scherzo no. 3 in c sharp
Chopin: Ballade no. 1 in g; Two Waltzes, in G flat and in A flat; Cham-
inade: *Automne;* Liszt: Hungarian Rhapsody no. 11; Schubert
arr. Tausig: *Marche militaire*

For most pianists, to present three such programs in the space of a week
would be exceptionally taxing. The repertoire embraces composers and
compositions familiar from Guerrero's previous concert programs, some
new composers (Rachmaninov), and some compositions he seems not to
have introduced in public before (Chopin's first Scherzo and first Ballade;
Liszt's *Rigoletto Fantasy* and *La campanella*). It also shows for the first time
a Beethoven sonata as an opener—notably not one of the major middle-
period sonatas but a subtler example.

At this youthful turning point in his career, Guerrero was not yet associated with eighteenth-century music—with Scarlatti or J.S. Bach or
Mozart—composers who were to be virtually his trademarks during his
later concerts in Canada. Another curious point is that, though commentators on his work in Chile mention specifically Arnold Schoenberg and Cyril
Scott as among the newer composers whose music he championed, none of
the surviving published programs include their music. Schoenberg's *Drei
Klavierstücke,* Opus 11, had been composed less than a decade earlier; we
have no exact idea of where or when Guerrero played this work in Chile.[19]
Nor do we know which of Scott's piano works, then considered highly
novel, he performed. Also missing from these and other programs that
have been preserved are any titles by Alexander Scriabin; the critical surveys
do not state that Guerrero played Scriabin's music, but its influence is dis-
cernable in his own compositions of the middle 1910s. He was identified as
an interpreter of Debussy and Ravel—though he incorporated a generous
amount of Debussy's piano music in his programs, the only Ravel work documented is *Jeux d'eau* (1901), for which however he had a lifelong fondness.

In the early months of 1918, after his Punta Arenas visit, Guerrero gave
further solo concerts in Santiago, Valparaíso, and Constitución, "which
attained great success."[20] He may have contributed to the programs of
the by-now-thriving Sociedad Bach around the same time.

On 31 May he gave a program of music by Debussy and Chopin, at
Santiago's Teatro Unión Central, partly as a memorial to Debussy, who had

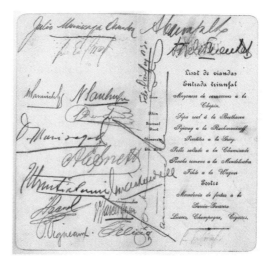

Menu, testimonial dinner, Punta Arenas, 12 January 1918 (Guerrero Collection)

died the previous 25 March. His brother Eduardo gave an introductory talk about Debussy and his music. The review in the next day's *Mercurio* was one of the few from Santiago sources to voice criticisms of Guerrero: "The distinguished pianist in a certain sense failed to convince us in his interpretations of Debussy"; but, among the Chopin numbers offered, the Études Opus 25 nos. 7 and 12 and the Scherzo (probably no. 3 in c sharp) "made a profound impression on the audience." The anonymous reviewer, though clearly well-read concerning Debussy's new and unfamiliar music, went on to admit: "Yesterday was the first time that we have attended a recital featuring six pieces by Debussy. The sustained applause elicited by the distinguished pianist's performances proves that the public accepts certain modern composers and listens to their music without the least show of displeasure—an attitude which says much in favour of our artistic culture."[21]

On 27 June in the Teatro Municipal came a "Grand Symphonic Concert: an expression of farewell to our eminent pianist Alberto García Guerrero." Uzcátegui refers to it as "one of the best [concerts] that has been heard in Santiago," and goes on to apply to Guerrero the words of a Spanish critic writing about Busoni: "no run-of-the-mill virtuoso, he is something else: a pianist of style, an exceptional interpreter whose nobility of interpretation reveals the soul of a great artist."[22]

The "Gran Concierto Sinfónico" promised an orchestra led by Juan Casanova Vicuña, with an assisting artist, the soprano Emita Ortiz, in the following program:

Beethoven	*Leonora* Overture no. 3
Wagner	"Elsa's dream," from *Lohengrin* (Ortiz)
Wagner	"Isolde's Love-Death," from *Tristan und Isolde* (Ortiz)
Chaikovski	Piano Concerto in b flat (Guerrero)
Chaikovski	*1812* Overture

In the event, Señora Ortiz "was unable to appear...being indisposed."[23] The deluxe printed program included an essay on Chaikovski's life, signed "Lily García Guerrero," in five lengthy paragraphs, two of them devoted to details of the composer's failed marriage ("su misterioso y desgraciado matrimonio"). The press comments on the event were highly favourable:

> We have seldom attended a more beautiful concert than that given yesterday in the [Teatro] Municipal. Alberto García Guerrero, the renowned pianist, and Juan Casanova Vicuña, the young "amateur" who assumed direction of the orchestra, performed their roles in brilliant fashion...García Guerrero showed the most complete precision in his playing of the Concerto, for which he was encored....This is the prestigious pianist's last appearance before our public, since he will soon leave for Canada to take over an important position offered to him by the management of the Hambourg Conservatory.[24]

An estimate of Guerrero's place among his musical contemporaries in Chile is afforded by the 1919 publication *Músicos chilenos contemporáneos* by the Ecuadorian critic Emilio Uzcátegui García, then resident in Chile.[25] This compilation of biographical notes on about two dozen performers and composers includes the following (figures indicate the length in pages of each article): Claudio Arrau ("el Mozart chileno"), 7; Armando Carvajal, 4; Rosita Renard, 8; Alberto García Guerrero, 10; Humberto Allende, 20; Enrique Soro, 22; Alfonso Leng Haygus, 6; Próspero Bisquertt, 7; Eliodoro Ortiz de Zárate, 22. Guerrero's prominent inclusion is based on the author's having heard him play in public several times and having interviewed him personally. Other biographies are of the leading composers—the respected older figure, Ortiz de Zárate; the main composition teachers, Allende and Soro; and the younger talents, Bisquertt and Leng. Guerrero's identity as a composer is underplayed.

Guerrero's multiple performing activities in Chile in this brief (eight-month) return are significant in two ways: the written and spoken responses denote the esteem of his colleagues which he had earned while still only comparatively young (thirty-two), and, in June, the reference to a "farewell" suggests he had announced his intention to leave Chile more or less permanently. The concert was a triumph, and the Guerreros made their departure from Chile with their ears ringing from some of the loudest tuttis in the orchestral repertoire.

Teatro Municipal

Jueves 27 de Junio de 1918
a las 6 P. M.

Gran Concierto Sinfónico

MANIFESTACIÓN DE DESPEDIDA
——— A ———
ALBERTO GARCÍA GUERRERO
NUESTRO EMINENTE PIANISTA

Con el Concurso de la notable soprano Sta. Emita Ortiz
y del Sr. Juan Casanova Vicuña, en la dirección de orquesta.

Program, "farewell" concert, Teatro Municipal, Santiago, 27 June 1918

On 7 May 1918 Boris, Mark Hambourg's brother, had written to Guerrero confirming his appointment (though money is not mentioned) as piano instructor at the Hambourg Conservatory in Toronto and as pianist of the Hambourg Trio in which Boris was the cellist and another brother, Jan, the violinist. The letter is in English and it reads, in part:

Dear Mr. Guerrero,

Following up our Telegram I am writing to say how pleased we are that you have decided to come and work with us in Toronto. We have been established here for nearly eight years and have worked up a big following both in Toronto and throughout the Dominion, as the School is well known from coast to coast....Of course we shall do all in our possibility to make you a success. Up to the present we succeeded in launching our Professors in the right way. In addition to your teaching we shall form a Trio, which I am sure will be an artistic pleasure to us all. I also expect you to have a couple of Programs ready, so that we can introduce you to the musical Public and our Students with recital and concert appearances.

Kindly send me the detailed Biography, stating where & when you were born; with whom studied etc. so that we should be able to print it in our Year Book, also please send plenty of Press notices several Photographs and a list of your printed compositions (if any). I would like you to arrive by the 1st or the 10th of August in Toronto, so as to get acquainted and settled down before your real work commences. We expect Jan Hambourg by that time from New York and we might start rehearsing our Trios for the following season.

With best compliments to your wife and yourself.[26]

This communication suggests that Guerrero had accepted the Toronto appointment some weeks before. The contractual "Telegram" mentioned has not surfaced. The return voyage via Panama to New York encountered signs of enemy action off Charleston. The ship, the *Suriname,* reached Ellis Island safely on 17 August and by late August, Alberto, Lily, and their tiny daughter were settled in a new life in Toronto.

Why?

Alberto Guerrero's story contains a central enigma: why did he give up his position as a front-ranking performer in Chile (referred to by his compatriots in the possessive—"*our* eminent pianist") in favour of a career in what might have justifiably been called a musical backwater like Toronto? And why, having done so, did he turn his back on family and friends in Chile and never return? Although the answer must be speculative, it can be based on a good deal of surrounding evidence.

Part of the answer may be purely economic. At this stage of his life, Guerrero faced family responsibilities, whereas previously he perhaps had never had to concern himself with even his own financial support.

Both the three-month tour of 1915–16 and the New York adventure could have led him to reconsider his place in the music world. A short but taxing experience of the life of a touring concert performer, followed by a period of freelance work in the intensely competitive surroundings of the metropolis, are likely to have left a sour taste. In later years, he would wonder out loud whether touring artists such as Claudio Arrau could possibly be happy with their lives. Arrau was a guest in Guerrero's home during several concert engagements in Toronto in the 1930s and '40s, where he would practise on Guerrero's piano. Guerrero admired Arrau but had no envy for his friend's constant travels away from his family and constant anxiety at having to keep his exceptionally large repertoire in fresh condition by practice. When pupils voiced their ambitions to enter the ranks of successful touring pianists, Guerrero would point out humanly preferable alternatives. For example, to the teenaged Ray Dudley, full of such ambitions, he spoke of the touring artist's life as a kind of prison, tied to repetitions of the same pieces and for long periods locked away from contact with friends and family. (Dudley nevertheless retained his ambitions, and fulfilled them in a fifty-year concert career about which he says "I believe I gave more concerts than any other Guerrero student, including Glenn [Gould]."[27])

Guerrero, it seems clear, discovered his own interests around this time, and decided to act on them. First, he enjoyed performing, enjoyed the exhilaration of big-audience fare but especially also the freedom to explore special areas of the repertoire beyond the big favourites. Second, he enjoyed solving technical problems, and was starting to develop an original approach to teaching. Indeed, he was ready to "discard all formal methods," when interviewed concerning his projected pedagogy manual. He was fascinated by the teaching process, and relished his own increasing mastery of it. Toronto afforded opportunities for a great deal of solo and group performing as well as a secure base for his development as a teacher. It seems that pedagogy became a passion alongside performing. These were the two strong professional motives leading to the satisfactions of his later years.

If this speculation suggests a new life pattern for him, it could have been realized equally well in Canada or in his faraway native country. But developments during the first decade of his new situation gradually reinforced his determination to remain in Canada.

three

Toronto: The Hambourgs

The Russian-Jewish musician Michael Hambourg (b. 1855) emigrated to Canada in 1910 and established the Hambourg Conservatory of Music in Toronto. A fixture of the local musical scene for almost half a century (it closed in 1951), the conservatory was housed in a sprawling mansion at the corner of Wellesley and Sherbourne Streets, with the homes of some of the city's wealthiest families immediately north in the Rosedale district and west on Jarvis Street, and with the more densely clustered middle-class residences of Cabbagetown to the east. (The building no longer stands.) Operated initially by Michael Hambourg, after his death in 1916 the school came under the direction of his sons, Jan, a violinist, and Boris, a cellist. An older son, Mark, was well established in a piano solo career in England, but made frequent visits to Canada, and was the original pianist of the family ensemble, the Hambourg Trio. A younger fourth son, Clement, never directly connected to the conservatory, was a freelance pianist, promoter, and, many years later, jazz entrepreneur. Jan eventually departed in 1920, leaving the conservatory administration in the hands of Boris and his wife Borina.[1]

Alberto Guerrero's appointment was auspicious, immediately announced in an interview in the Toronto *Sunday World* on 28 August. The interview was conducted in French, Guerrero's second language; evidently his stay in New York had not yet given him the fluency in English he later acquired.[2] He liked Toronto, he said, and found the climate so far agreeable. This led to comments about his native country for comparison: "We have all climates in Chile; it is a narrow country, but very long, reaching far south. Punta Arenas, the southern-most city in the world, I believe, where I have played, is in Chile." The long boat voyage also came in for comment:

> Señor Guerrero told us that as long as they were on the Pacific all was well....At Colón [Panama], however, the voyage became more eventful; countless papers that long (an expansive splay of arms illustrated this) had to be signed and endorsed;...the red-tape was endless. From Charleston up, the coast was guarded by patrol boats, and a submarine had been sighted there the day before....The very next night they saw a ship on fire, its brilliant blaze staring at them through the black night...she had been torpedoed. After that, there was frequent drilling and coaching in the adjustment of life preservers, in manoeuvres with lifeboats, and other activities in case of peril, until the haven of New York was finally reached in safety.[3]

Musical and artistic topics formed a minor part of the conversation, though when asked his views on aesthetic trends, Guerrero stressed the importance of Debussy. The article ends: "I knew that the distinguished pianist must be still fatigued with travelling, and that moreover he was to play that night."

Immediately on his arrival, in fact, Guerrero was conscripted for performances with the Hambourgs in their week-long series of "soirées musicales" at the King Edward Hotel. For Monday's program, there was "a slight disappointment at the non-appearance of Alberto García Guerrero, the noted Chilean pianist, who missed his train in New York and did not arrive in time." Gerald Moore substituted for him in the piano part of Arensky's Trio in d. On the Tuesday, Guerrero joined the others in Beethoven's Trio in c, Opus 1, no. 3, and "played himself into the hearts of a Toronto audience" which included "many men, a notable number being in khaki." He "at once left no doubt as to his being in the very front rank of virtuoso pianists." For Wednesday's soirée, he offered a considerable solo group: Debussy's *Jardins sous la pluie* and *L'isle joyeuse;* Liszt's *Rigoletto Fantasy;* and Chopin's Scherzo no. 3 in c sharp, Berceuse, and Polonaise in A flat, earning the critical judgment "a masterly pianist."[4]

Among pupils of his first year or two at the Hambourgs' were several who became prominent professionals: Reginald Stewart as an orchestral conductor in Toronto and Baltimore, Gerald Moore as a piano accompanist to some of the principal European singers of the mid-century, and Edward Magee and Margaret Clemens as active performers and teachers in Toronto. A letter from Mrs. Hambourg Sr, dated 10 May 1921, thanks Guerrero for the benefit her young son Clement has derived from his piano studies. Public recitals either entirely or mainly by pianists from Guerrero's studio took place in 1919 on 12 April, 10 and 29 May, and 7 October. At the October event, in Massey Hall, a reviewer reveals that

Moore "is shortly going to Europe to study."[5] Clemens played a Haydn Sonata, and is described as "a little mite who could scarcely reach the pedal." There were similar presentations in 1920 and 1921, often introducing concerti in which Guerrero would play the orchestral part on a second piano. There was an entire two-piano program by half a dozen of his pupils in Massey Hall on 6 December 1921.

His teaching may have been a main preoccupation, but appearances on the concert stage are mentioned starting soon after his arrival. There was a solo "début" concert in Massey Hall and a solo recital for the Women's Musical Club of Toronto at the Masonic Hall, both in December 1918; a solo recital in London, Ontario, in January 1919; a shared program with Winifred Hicks-Lyne, mezzo-soprano, in Toronto, and concerts with the Hambourg Trio, in Toronto and also in London, later that year.

Massey Hall, Toronto's main location for classical music presentations from 1894 through 1982, and still a distinguished older venue in the downtown area, had a seating capacity of 4,000 prior to the renovations in 1933—which makes it a surprising choice for a solo concert by a newly arrived and little-known pianist or for a group of his advanced students. For Guerrero's so-called début on 2 December, his program consisted of the Bach-Busoni Prelude and Fugue in D, Beethoven's Écossaises and *Turkish March,* Chopin's Sonata no. 2 in b flat, Debussy's *L'isle joyeuse,* Guerrero's own *Capricho* and *Vals triste,* a Concert Etude by MacDowell, and two pieces by Liszt—*Au bord d'une source* and the Polonaise in E. "The recital...attracted a very large audience, and the warmth of his reception was such as is accorded to but few visiting pianists....The wide range of his program revealed his versatility and intellectual grasp of big subjects...complete mastery...uncommon artistic attainments."[6] Besides covering a "wide range," the program was in some respects quite unconventional: for example, in representing Beethoven not by a sonata but by the delightful chain of six dances (WoO. 83) and the march from his *Ruins of Athens* music—both probably in arrangements. For the WMC concert on 19 December, the lineup repeated the MacDowell and *L'isle joyeuse* and included an unspecified Beethoven sonata and further pieces by Debussy (*Pagodes, Jardins sous la pluie* and *La cathédrale engloutie*). The contralto Winifred Parker was assisting artist. The London solo concert, 22 January 1919, drew either "a large attendance" or an "array of empty seats," depending on which newspaper you read.[7] Under a sub-heading "Is He Left-Handed?" the *Advertiser*'s reviewer commented that "few artists have been heard who have developed to such a high degree their left hand technique. [Guerrero] didn't include a left hand study in his program, but one could imagine an unusual presentation had this been the case." Guerrero was right-handed.

The Hambourg Trio (as the "Hambourg Concert Society") presented a season of four concerts in the Foresters' Hall on College Street, to which Guerrero was a regular contributor. On 11 February, besides the Schumann Trio, he performed a solo group (Alkan's *Le vent,* Opus 15, no. 2, Ravel's *Jeux d'eau,* and Albéniz's *Triana*); Gerald Moore was the accompanist for a solo group by Jan Hambourg on that program. On 11 March, departing from the usual recital format, Boris Hambourg presented a spoken survey of "the history of the pianoforte and its literature," for which Guerrero played the most wide-ranging selection of works he had ever done up to that point: examples by Purcell, Couperin, Rameau, Bach, Scarlatti, Haydn, Mozart, and Beethoven in the "classical" group; Schubert, Schumann, Mendelssohn, Chopin, and Liszt in the "romantic"; and Rachmaninov, Alkan, Debussy, and Albéniz in the "modern." That he was rapidly adding new items to his repertoire at this period is obvious. The music of Valentin Alkan (1813–88) was so different from that of his romantic-era contemporaries that it counted as "modern." In the shared program of 26 March, also at the Foresters', Guerrero played Debussy's *Reflets dans l'eau* and Franck's Prelude, Chorale, and Fugue, the latter a cornerstone work of his entire concert career. On 8 April he repeated the Franck and joined the Hambourgs in Beethoven's Opus 1, no. 3 and the *Dumky* Trio by Dvořák. On 14 May, a "request program," the featured works were the Rachmaninov Cello Sonata (Boris Hambourg and Guerrero) and Beethoven's *Archduke* Trio in B flat, Opus 97. On 6 November, Guerrero and Jan Hambourg presented a joint recital in Ottawa, at St. Patrick's Hall, sponsored by the Morning Musical Club. Guerrero's solo numbers were ones he had recently introduced in Toronto: *L'isle joyeuse, Le vent,* and *Triana.* The duos offered were Schubert's Sonatina Opus 137 and the Sonata Opus 24 by Sylvio Lazzari (1857–1944), a now largely forgotten disciple of Franck.

The trio's well-advertised concert in New York's Aeolian Hall took place on 5 January 1920. The reviews centred on the novelty of the program, the US premiere of the Trio in f sharp, Opus 30, by the contemporary Belgian composer Joseph Jongen. The work, whose cello part was originally written for the viola, received a repeat performance the same evening in New York by a rival concert association—a coincidence making for good copy. "It was Eugène Ysaÿe...who urged [the Hambourg Trio] to incorporate the work of his compatriot in their repertory, even though the viola were replaced by a cello."[8] Ysaÿe had been one of Jan Hambourg's teachers. The Lazzari violin sonata and Beethoven's *Ghost* Trio in D, Opus 70, no. 1, completed the New York program. Press comments were sufficiently "mixed," evidently, to discourage the group's investment in further New York appearances.

The Hambourg Trio

JAN HAMBOURG, - - - Violinist,
ALBERTO GARCIA GUERRERO, Pianist,
BORIS HAMBOURG, - - - 'Cellist.

For Dates, Terms, Etc.—Apply to Loudon Charlton, Carnegie Hall, New
York, or Secretary, The Hambourg Trio, 194 Wellesley Street, Toronto.

Concert brochure, Hambourg Trio, 1920
(Guerrero Collection)

On 26 January, Boris Hambourg and Guerrero repeated their illus-
trated "history of the pianoforte" in Convocation Hall at Queen's University, Kingston, Ontario. Though sketchier and more global in content, the
presentation appears reminiscent of the Chilean lecture-recitals given in collaboration with his brother years before. As evidence of a certain social
attainment, an undated clipping of 1920 records a supper at the home of
Sir Edmund Walker "in honor of Señor and Madame Guerrero," attended
by leading musical figures of Toronto such as Paul Wells, Viggo Kihl, Luigi
von Kunits, Healey Willan, and Augustus S. Vogt—with, one gathers, their
spouses. There remained a few titled personages among the Toronto intel-
ligentsia at this period; Walker (1848–1924) was a prominent banker, art
collector, and philanthropist.

The 1920–21 series of three "Tuesday nine o'clocks" at Jenkins Art Galleries featured the Hambourg Trio along with the English baritone James
Campbell-McInnes who was, like Guerrero, a new arrival on the Toronto
musical scene.[9] Campbell-McInnes's accompanist was George Reeves. On
23 November the trio played Haydn's "Gypsy Rondo" Trio and the new
Jongen work; on 14 December Guerrero joined Jan Hambourg in
Beethoven's *Kreutzer* Sonata in A, Opus 47, and the trio played John Ire-

land's Trio no. 2 in c. On 4 January 1921, the instrumental items were Léon Boëllmann's Cello Sonata, Opus 40 (Boris Hambourg and Guerrero) and the Dvořák *Dumky* Trio. On 29 November the three performers had travelled to Utica in Upper New York State for a concert at the New Century Club Auditorium, the program consisting of repeats: the trios by Dvořák and Haydn, plus the *Kreutzer.*

A large undated newspaper advertisement, apparently from 1920, is evidence of yet another outlet for the hard-working young performer: at the Allen motion-picture theatre, Richmond and Victoria Streets (later renamed the Tivoli), there would be an "Engagement Extraordinary" of "Alberto Guerrero, the celebrated South American pianist, in repertoire." This probably indicates a week's engagement calling for two or three short daily "sets," whether solo or with the house orchestra is unknown. The theatre's music director at the time was Luigi Romanelli.

Letters from Lily and Alberto Guerrero to his former associates in Chile stimulated articles in the musical press there reporting on his North American successes. The Hambourg Conservatory's thriving program and emphasis on piano instruction made a marked impression:

> As music educator, the Chilean artist has roused at the conservatory a positive reaction in which we should all take pride. He has more than four hundred pupils and thirty piano teachers under his supervision, and the number of pupils will probably be augmented with more recent registrations to over five hundred. He has been obliged to divide his time carefully between his classes and the preparation of his public solo and trio recitals.[10]

These busy new enterprises and responsibilities were interrupted by tragic news. Eduardo García Guerrero, the brother with whom Guerrero always had closest ties, died in Santiago on 20 March, 1919. He was thirty-five years old. The obituary notice in *El Mercurio* speaks of his final illness as "short" and "surprising," and portrays him as a distinguished and versatile public figure:

> His lectures on music, where he illuminated fully and learnedly the performances of his brother Alberto; his studies in penal and judicial sociology; his extensive political action with the Centro Liberal, of which he was president and whose activities he aided through speeches and articles; a public servant, hard-working and exceptionally well-prepared, above all in his duties as librarian of the External Affairs department—in every area he leaves a deeply imprinted record of his life and of his generous efforts....Modest and sensitive, whoever saw him in the battles of daily life would hardly guess at the highly interesting abilities of this young man, gifted, despite his youth, of so much culture and proverbial kindness.[11]

The specific cause of Eduardo's death is not stated; one biographical notice gives a hint only of the "battles" he had to contend with: "suddenly his life was cut short, destroyed by the misfortune of his alcoholic tendencies."[12] This major family loss may have strengthened Guerrero's decision to pursue his new life in Canada rather than accepting offers to return to Chile.

The Guerreros lived close to the conservatory in their first Toronto years, first at 413 Sherbourne Street, then (from 1920 to 1923) at 59A-197 Wellesley Street, immediately opposite, and still later in Cabbagetown locations—first at 24 Prospect Avenue (1923–25), then (from 1925) at 25 Winchester Street. Guerrero did not own a car. All these residences were within walking distance of the Hambourg Conservatory—or within a short streetcar ride of the Toronto Conservatory of Music, with which he was affiliated starting in 1922.

The TCM (since 1947 known as the Royal Conservatory of Music) had grown since its founding by Edward Fisher in the year of Guerrero's birth, 1886, to a position of major eminence not just for Toronto but for Canada at large. Registrations for private music lessons locally reached into the thousands, and its nationwide examination system, after the models of British schools such as the Royal Academy of Music and Trinity College, London, came to have a benchmark function in musical education in both performance and theory throughout Canada. In 1921, the year before Guerrero's contract began, it came under the management of the University of Toronto, and shortly afterwards, in 1924, absorbed its main rival, the Canadian Academy of Music, becoming even more dominant.

The Hambourg Conservatory, by contrast, retained its smaller independent character. Guerrero's position there initially had combined teaching and a certain amount of administration with trio performances. On Jan Hambourg's 1920 departure for a career in the USA and Europe, his role as violinist was taken over by Henri Czaplinski. A concert in Sault Ste. Marie, Ontario, on 25 October 1921, introduced Czaplinski in a program including Schubert's Trio in E flat, Opus 100, and there were concerts in Massey Hall on 4 February, 4 March, and 1 April the following year. The main ensemble works presented were by Schubert, Brahms, and Chaikovski, and Guerrero wound up the final program with a performance of the first movement of the Chaikovski Concerto in b flat (his pupil Eva Galloway Farmer played the orchestral part on a second piano). But, although Boris Hambourg remained a leading figure in several chamber-music ensembles in Toronto in ensuing years, notably the Hart House String Quartet, specific and ongoing prospects for Guerrero's skill and experience in this area were, temporarily at least, curtailed as the trio's activities became less frequent.[13]

This may have increased the appeal of an invitation to join the TCM, where he was rapidly signed on for concerts with the Conservatory Trio— Frank Blachford, violin, Leo Smith, cello—and, a few seasons later, with the Conservatory String Quartet. Blachford was a Canadian educated in Germany, while the English-born Smith had performed in orchestras under Hans Richter, Arthur Nikisch, and the composers Elgar and Debussy in Britain prior to taking up residence in Canada. Smith's fellow artists in the quartet were Elie Spivak and Harold Sumberg, violins, and Donald Heins, viola.

Guerrero was active as a solo performer. A solo recital at an unspecified Toronto location on 26 April 1921 had included an arrangement of Debussy's *L'après-midi d'un faune* and, in what may have been its concert première, Guerrero's own Tango. A reviewer remarked: "Mr Guerrero has an idiomatic style. He is always enormously interesting," but added more acidly, "His own tango nobody could tango to, and his *Valse Triste* sounded like Cyril Scott lost on the Andes."[14]

A solo program for the Art and Music Club in Grant Hall, Kingston, Ontario, on 19 January 1922, strikes a new and prophetic chord: it consists exclusively of classical keyboard works—by Scarlatti, Couperin, J.S. Bach (the *Chromatic Fantasia and Fugue*), Haydn (Variations in f), Mozart (Sonata in G, K.283), and Beethoven (the *Appassionata* Sonata in f, Opus 57). Here is evidence that Guerrero was pursuing the "history of the pianoforte" more deeply than ever before. His solo concert at the TCM on 7 February 1924 included two major classics, Beethoven's *Waldstein* Sonata, Opus 53, and Brahms's Variations on a Theme by Paganini. A year later, 2 April 1925, in another TCM solo appearance, he juxtaposed Haydn, Beethoven, and Schumann works with examples from his Debussy repertoire.

Simultaneously with his classical probings, he seems to have continued to investigate the newer music from Europe. For example, on 28 March 1923, he collaborated with the Argentinian pianist Carlos Buhler in a program of music for two pianos that included Debussy's *En blanc et noir* and Germaine Tailleferre's *Jeux de plein air*, and in another recital shortly afterwards, 6 June 1923, he and his juvenile pupil Audrey Maunder repeated the Tailleferre. His joint recital at the TCM with the violinist Ferdinand Fillion, 12 December 1923, included sonatas by Debussy and Milhaud. Guerrero may well have been responsible for giving Toronto audiences their first taste of music by the "Les Six" members Milhaud and Tailleferre.

Toronto in the 1920s has been depicted in novels and memoirs as culturally narrow-minded and puritanical, a bastion of WASP abstinence, symbolized by the drawn curtains on the Eaton's department store show-

Fifteenth Concert

Sunday, March 16th, 1924

———

PROGRAMME

C. Franck	Prelude, Chorale et Fugue
Debussy	Jardins sous la pluie
	Voiles
	La Cathedrale engloutie
	L'Isle Joyeuse
Albeniz	El Puerto
Dubois	Les Abeilles
Saint-Saens	Etude en forme de Valse

Signor Guerrero, Pianist

Heintzman Piano used

Program, solo concert by Alberto Guerrero, Great Hall, Hart House, University of Toronto, 16 March 1924

windows on Sundays. This view is hardly borne out in contemporary memoirs concerning the arts, from which we learn, for example, that a vital art community thrived in the quasi-bohemian area around Gerrard and Bay streets, and that vaudeville and playhouse performances regularly took place at a dozen downtown theatres. In 1923, when a "New Symphony Orchestra" rose from the ashes of the disbanded Toronto Symphony Orchestra (1906–18), it was led by the Austrian-born Luigi von Kunits, whose students—gifted children of immigrants from Eastern Europe— occupied most desks in the string section. The new ensemble, taking up its predecessor's name in 1925, performed its concerts in the late afternoon so that its members could get to their regular jobs in the pit bands of the silent-movie houses by evening. Guerrero was soloist in the Schumann Concerto with this orchestra on 28 October 1924. (On 15 January of the same year, the young Colin McPhee had created a *succès de scandale* as soloist in his own Concerto no. 2.)[15]

On 8 April 1923, during the second season of the Sunday Evening Concerts series in the Great Hall of Hart House, the social centre of the University of Toronto, Guerrero and Buhler played a shortened version of their piano-duo program given a few weeks earlier at the TCM. This was the first of many appearances Guerrero was to make in the Hart House series, participating either as solo pianist or as chamber music performer almost every year until 1952: there were, for example, solo recitals at Hart House on 16 March 1924 and 18 January 1925, a joint concert with his pupil Edward Magee on 31 October 1926, and so on. He was also a frequent performer in the Friday noon series in the Hart House music room, and soon became well-known and respected on the university campus.

An anonymous review in the Montreal *Star* suggests that he played at least one concert in that city around this period.[16]

Guerrero began giving broadcast recitals in those years when music on the radio was still a pioneering venture: he was heard in 1924 playing on local stations in Toronto, Montreal, New York City, Utica, Schenectady, and Philadelphia. His hour-long recital on 2 April elicited the following technical appreciation:

> A combination of a pianist of such fame and ability as Guerrero, favorable atmospheric conditions and excellent transmission, made CFCA's recital...one of the best in its recent history.
>
> Signor [*sic*] Guerrero...is one of the leading pianists of the continent. He has revealed his wisdom still further by studying closely the effect of radio transmission in piano music, with the result that a radio piano recital by him gives a thrill of artistic delight.
>
> ...Listener after listener telephoned to *The Star* to say that it was just as if Signor Guerrero was in their house playing at that moment....Several...commented...that the quality of Guerrero's playing was much deeper and richer than piano music which came in last night from Chicago, St. Louis, and other stations.
>
> Signor Guerrero will be playing next week on the radio from Montreal and the following week from New York.[17]

The radio program started with Chopin's Ballade no. 1 in g and ended with Debussy's *L'isle joyeuse*. In between were other pieces by Chopin, Mendelssohn, and Saint-Saens. Perhaps the same works made up the programs in Montreal on 8 April and in New York (WEAF) on 17 April. A columnist in the Toronto *Star* announced that among the features radio fans could tune in was an address by President Calvin Coolidge:

> Coolidge to Speak Tuesday Evening.
> – Being Broadcast by Chain of American Stations.
> – Guerrero, Too.
>
> From the Waldorf-Astoria in New York Tuesday evening April 22, President Coolidge will speak about 8:30. From WEAF, New York, at 9:45 the same evening Signor [*sic*] Guerrero of Toronto will give one of his famous piano recitals for radio. He has given recitals of this kind from The *Star*, from Montreal, and from Schenectady.[18]

The *Star* owned station CFCA, which partly explains the generous space given to advance listings and reviews of the programs. A Philadelphia journalist, identified as "the Old Timer," commented:

When an artist of first rank cuts loose on the piano and this instrument is "microphoned" as perfectly as through WGY, the result is bound to be a wonderful performance. Alberto Guerrero gave a recital there recently, and it seemed as though he were right in my living room....The pianist ought to get a flood of applause for such a performance.[19]

In either late 1924 or early 1925, Ferdinand Fillion and Guerrero broadcast César Franck's Violin Sonata in A from Schenectady, and "several hundred letters of appreciation were received."[20] They had presented this work on the concert stage "on several [previous] occasions," but clearly the radio performance had a novel impact.

In the days before magnetic tape recording, programs were preserved, if at all, on sixteen-inch transcription discs. A diligent search of radio archives has so far discovered no transcription recordings of Guerrero's recitals from this period. These bellwether activities prefigure his prominence in CBC network broadcasts in the 1940s; from these likewise, regrettably, there are no extant recordings.

Leading pupils in Guerrero's first TCM years were Horace Lapp, a versatile composer-improviser, and theatre and radio musician, and Audrey Maunder, a spectacular pre-teen talent. Edward Magee, Margaret Clemens, Eva Galloway Farmer, and Adele Doney, all from his Hambourg Conservatory years, appear to have continued studying with him. Maunder's performance of the first movement of Beethoven's Concerto no. 3 in c, at Massey Hall on 28 May 1924, as part of a conservatory term-end concert by students, drew special comment: "Audrey Maunder, a frail little miss of some 10 years, astonished her hearers....Her octave runs, taken at a sprightly tempo, were a revelation."[21] Margaret Clemens, who had occupied the position of moppet-in-residence at the Hambourgs', gave impressive full recitals in the TCM Concert Hall in 1923 and again in 1925, representing Guerrero's studio.

After settling in Toronto, Guerrero was clearly active in most of his previous specialties, save for composition. Where his composing of the last ten years or so in Chile shows an increase in diversity and in experimentation, there are virtually no original works from his first ten years in Canada, and those few pieces he produced later were pleasant genre studies for piano pupils rather than original concert works. He was not designated a "pianist-composer" or "composer-pianist" during his Canadian years, as he had been in Chile and in New York. The reasons may be twofold. First, at some point he evidently gave up thinking of himself as a creative musician, made no effort to preserve his earlier music, and may indeed have destroyed a good deal of it—although he did not abandon his keen interest in what other composers were doing. Second, there was also little recognition of local composers in Canada in the 1920s and '30s, and no concerted movement aimed at fostering their work. As early as 1915, the Canadian composer Wesley Octavius Forsyth had commented sarcastically: "It is not considered elsewhere (the United States, England, and on the continent of Europe, etc.) a weakness to patronize and to recognize the honest efforts of their native composers."[22] The conductor von Kunits, himself the composer of a violin concerto and several substantial chamber works, viewed the performance of music by Canada's, and Toronto's, composers as a marginal duty at best:

> Among the great contemporary composers, those of the European continent are still considered to be the leading ones. Canadian and American writers occupy, as yet, a secondary place. Works of Canadian and American composers should then, principally, be performed for the sake of national encouragement; and, from this standpoint, even local composers might be recognized, whenever their writings show a sufficient degree of merit.[23]

El cónsul

Through almost the entire 1920s, and intermittently later, Guerrero devoted part of his busy schedule to duties unconnected with music: he served as honorary consul for Chile from 1921 to 1928. He was a well-known personality in his homeland and, despite his growing feelings of severance, he apparently felt no objection to helping Chilean nationals visiting Toronto, or Torontonians seeking Chilean contacts. The responsibilities were light (there was no consulate staff in Toronto until 1979 or '80, and the office opened at its present central location in 1998) and, however modest the remuneration, he and his family enjoyed the advantage of diplomatic travel papers. He was referred to as "special honorary consul" ("Cónsul Particular Honorario").

Documents in the files of the Chilean ministry of foreign affairs provide details.[24] On 27 October 1921 the Chilean embassy in London acknowledges receipt from the ministry of letters patent naming "Señor García Guerrero" as consul in Toronto. On 1 January the following year, the embassy's annual report lists changes of personnel in the various consulates under its jurisdiction, of which it mentions four in the United Kingdom and nine in the British "dominions and colonies," including two in Canada (one in Amherst, Nova Scotia, and one in Toronto). Guerrero's name appears with the last of these.

Six years later, on 2 February 1928, the ministry complained that it had received no annual report from Guerrero, despite repeated reminders; the supervisor in London suggested replacing him if he did not respond. By

4 April, with still no response, the ministry recommended that the supervisor start thinking of a suitable replacement. On 28 August, it appears Lily Wilson Guerrero had written explaining that her husband had been "absent" ("ausente") and therefore unable to fulfill his consular duties. She asked to be named consul in his place. The ministry replied tartly: "the department does not find it convenient, at this time, to name women as consuls of Chile"—and ordered that someone else be appointed in Guerrero's stead. The name of Ernest Fergus Whitelaw, an accountant with Schmietendorf and Co., was proposed. Guerrero meanwhile (26 September) "promised the Department in future to exercise the best possible dedication and zeal in carrying out his duties," and was defended as "a distinguished Chilean, honoured both in our country and abroad." In case Guerrero could not effectively meet the hopes the ministry had placed in him, Whitelaw was again suggested. On 8 November 1928 "Ernesto Fergus Whitelaw" was named consul-elect, replacing Guerrero.

His teaching, performing, and travel assignments during those years were indeed heavy, which would explain why he might neglect the few duties expected of him as consul, though not why he was described as "absent." His was not the temperament of an administrator, much less that of a "boss." He exerted authority efficiently but quietly. Associates and pupils regarded him as a guru who extended advice rather than as a manager who gave orders. In the large family he grew up in, he was no doubt more accustomed to taking orders than to giving them. Would such a temperament be the underlying reason for his apparent lapses in this area?

In any case, all was forgiven. Information from the general archives of the Chilean ministry of foreign affairs outlines his later reinstatement: "[Guerrero] was appointed 'special consul-elect' (Cónsul Particular de Elección) on 29 February 1932, serving in this capacity until 1934. On 12 February 1935 he was named 'honorary consul,' and held this post until [the end of] 1938. During 1939 we had no consulate. It reopened in 1940 with another Consul, who served until 1942, at which date the consulate was closed until its establishment in 1979."[25]

Personal Crises

The temporary misunderstandings over a minor position with the consular service, and Lily Guerrero's part in trying to solve them, may signal deeper difficulties that in 1928 were beginning to threaten the family and, in particular, the marriage. Lily's position was awkward, and her abilities to adapt as a Spanish-speaking Catholic woman to a new cultural environment seem to have been seriously challenged. Though Guerrero quickly mastered English, Spanish was the language of their home: their daughter

Left to right: unidentified, Lily Wilson Guerrero, Edward ("Weedy") Magee, ca. 1928 (Collection M. Irvine)

grew up fluently bilingual, speaking English at her separate (Catholic) school, St. Joseph's Academy, and Spanish with her parents. Lily's background in upper-class circles in Chile had given her expensive tastes, and these are said to have placed a strain on the family budget. The family had a maid, but only "when Daddy (i.e., Guerrero) could afford it," says Mélisande Irvine. Both partners were attractive and personable: there were rumours of flirtations and possible infidelities on both sides. There were further changes of residence—to no. 306, 106 Maitland Street, in 1929, and again to no. 10, 72 Isabella Street, in 1931. (These addresses are all in the same central part of Toronto.)

By 1931, they had arranged to separate. Lily and Mélisande, then in her early teens, returned to Santiago. After a few years they relocated first to Paris and then to Brussels. While in Europe, Mélisande completed secondary school and then attended art school. Guerrero continued to support his family, and during his summer trips to Europe in the mid-1930s maintained contact with his daughter.[26] While he accepted that the marriage was over, it seems clear that Lily did not. Whether a Catholic attitude or wounded family pride was responsible, she refused to consider a divorce that would have freed Guerrero to marry Myrtle Rose, the young pupil with whom he had by this time begun a new relationship. Under Canadian law at the time, adultery was the only accepted grounds for divorce, and it was up to the "aggrieved spouse" to initiate the action. Rare in Canadian society, divorce was almost unheard of in Chile.

In January 1934, Lily wrote from Santiago, on black-edged notepaper, announcing the death of "poor Daniel" on Christmas night. (She enclosed the obituary notices.) Dr. Daniel García Guerrero was mourned as "the outstanding figure in internal medicine in Chile."[27] Guerrero's oldest brother was sixty-six years of age. His passing was a reminder of the lessons he had supervised in Alberto's childhood, and of their joint musical activities in Santiago in the 1910s. Alberto, the youngest, was now the only surviving brother of the illustrious García Guerrero trio. That the news came from Lily is an indication she considered it proper to maintain her wifely status at this time.

In 1932 or early 1933 Guerrero moved again, from Isabella Street to the apartment at 51 Grosvenor Street which was to be his home for the next twenty years. After the first year or two, he leased, in addition to the fourth-floor apartment itself, the penthouse studio above it, and here he housed his pianos—a Steinway and an Ibach—and did all his teaching, practising, and rehearsing. A large, bright room with windows facing east, south, and west, it was always referred to as "the sunroom." (The four-and-a-half-storey building still stood in the early 2000s.) Myrtle Rose had a smaller apartment at the same address. Grosvenor was their joint home, although they were obliged to disguise the fact in various transparent ways, such as renting two different flats. It was many years before they were able to marry.

Myrtle Rose was born in North Battleford, Saskatchewan, 5 August 1906, and received her early education in Lethbridge, Alberta. She came to Toronto in 1928 to study music at the TCM, first with Peter Kennedy and then with Guerrero. Their intimacy seems to have started in mid-1931. It is difficult to determine whether it was the main cause of the marriage breakdown: certainly it was a contributing factor. Myrtle was young, strikingly beautiful, and talented; she also shared with Guerrero a deep interest in, and understanding of, music. Their bond, however impulsive it may have been at the start, was not long in finding lasting and secure foundations. Moreover, it was tacitly acknowledged and accepted by all but the most blinkered or censorious of their colleagues. Another misconception of social historians concerning Toronto in those years is that unconventional relationships were universally frowned on. This could be refuted not only by Rose and Guerrero but by half a dozen other situa-

Myrtle Rose, piano student, ca. 1930
(Guerrero Collection)

tions—adulterous as well as same-sex unions—which were then equally well-known and well-accepted in the musical community, and a number of others in the artistic community at large.

Toronto: The Late 1920s and Early '30s; The TCM

Toronto was a different musical milieu from the one Guerrero had known in Santiago. Far from the emphasis being on Italian opera, there *was* no opera, whether Italian or not; and far from any lack of organized choral and orchestral events, these were a regular and much-cultivated feature. The powers in the city's professional-music scene were either instrumentalists like von Kunits, the Hambourgs, and Leo Smith, or choirmaster-organists like Healey Willan, Albert Ham, Herbert A. Fricker, Richard Tattersall, Thomas J. Crawford, and Augustus Stephen Vogt. All of these choirmaster-organists were recent arrivals from England or Scotland, with the exception of Vogt, a native Canadian from a German background. The rise during the 1920s of the brilliant Ernest MacMillan was partly due to his reconciliation of these two strands—a Canadian born from Scottish roots, and a gifted organist and choir director, he was also active as a composer, conductor, and chamber-music pianist. By his personal charisma and extraordinary energy he gradually assumed the main leadership positions in education and performance, not only in Toronto but virtually of the whole country. On Vogt's death in 1926 it was almost automatic that MacMillan would take over his dual position as principal of the TCM and dean of the University of Toronto Faculty of Music. After von Kunits died in 1931 it was MacMillan who succeeded him as conductor of the Toronto Symphony Orchestra; in 1938 the pattern repeated once more when, at Fricker's passing, MacMillan assumed the directorship of the city's largest choral organization, the Toronto Mendelssohn Choir. He and Guerrero became frequent collaborators, and good friends.

Guerrero's position in Toronto's social round was that of a quiet, purposeful maker of music. At the larger school, he had fewer administrative responsibilities than in his Hambourg post, although the records show him as a long-serving member of the TCM's advisory "board of studies" (1936–53) and he took part every season in the annual rounds of practical examinations both in Toronto and on tour in various parts of the country. His daughter remembers that every June he would be "on the road" as an examiner—mainly, he said, "because it paid well."[28] He put in his first examining stint shortly after his appointment in the early 1920s, and his last, evidently, in 1951.[29] His teaching fees were among the best at the TCM, but fees generally were not high in that period, so the extra earnings to be expected from a term of duty as an examiner were hard to resist.

The TCM local-centre examination circuit is acknowledged to have special importance in Canadian music education. Given the vast dispersal of the population, the visits of leading professionals to small towns in all regions for one-on-one contact with young music students were a vital factor in the establishment of standards. Their success depended on the willing participation of those "leading professionals"—it was not unusual for a lineup of ten-year-old hopefuls in, say, Swift Current, Saskatchewan, to present their pianistic abilities for the scrutiny of a MacMillan or a Kihl or a Guerrero. The examiner often lingered for consultations or a master class with the local teachers: the teachers' courses given by Guerrero in the summers of 1931 and 1932 in Saskatoon and Edmonton are an example. The Saskatoon course lasted a month (6 July to 1 August) and was preceded by a solo recital; the shorter Edmonton presentation the following year (when there were over a hundred examination candidates in piano) appears to have been equally well-received.[30]

Guerrero's earnings from teaching and examining for the TCM in 1924–25 totalled $2,412.53.[31] Tuition fees were published in the conservatory's year books starting only in 1940–41. Guerrero's fee was then $45 for ten half-hour lessons or $81 for ten one-hour lessons. Whether he ever taught in half-hour segments is unlikely; certainly in later years he did not, and the allocation of an hour often stretched well beyond that limit.

The violinist Kathleen Parlow, appointed in 1941–42, was available only for terms of ten one-hour lessons, at $100; Guerrero's fee remained the same that season, and in every season up until 1948–49, when the rate for ten half-hour lessons increased to $55. Other major piano instructors on the conservatory's roster—Viggo Kihl, Ernest Seitz, Lubka Kolessa—charged slightly higher fees. Rates were set not by the administration but by the individual teachers. Guerrero appears at the top of the tuition-fee list for the first time in 1949–50, alongside the newcomers Boris Roubakine and Béla Bösörmenyi-Nagy (Kihl had died in 1945, Seitz had resigned in 1946 and Kolessa in 1949, notably transforming the piano-teaching scene). In 1953–54, rather than raising the rates for tuition across the board, the conservatory lowered the number of lessons constituting a "term," to nine instead of ten. In 1958–59, Guerrero's second-last season of teaching, his fee for nine half-hours rose to $60. In practical terms, this indicates that at the end of his career, he was available to a private student for just under $500 a year.[32]

The early TCM years yield few literary contributions by Guerrero. His colleague Leo Smith, author and critic as well as cellist, edited the house journal, called variously the *Conservatory Bi-Monthly, Monthly,* or *Quarterly.* From the early 1930s we find a brief critical entry entitled "Promenade" by Guerrero, essentially a selection of *aperçus* from his teaching and performing experience. It ends with this "Advice to Myself":

Do not put in the expression, the music has it.

Play every note.

Give each note the value written, and an intensity of sound proportionate to its place in the rhythm, in the melody, in the harmony.

Follow the directions of the composer. He made the composition. You are just playing it. The listeners will reconstruct it as they please, or, better, as they can.—And by all means leave the emotion to them. They have nothing else to attend to.[33]

This suggests an intellectual rigour bordering on arrogance. His attitude to his hearers and also to the role of emotion in music softened in later life. But his ideals of objectivity and honesty in performance remained.

While initially teaching in a studio in the TCM building at College Street and University Avenue, Guerrero at length found he preferred to meet with pupils in his own apartment-studio, and henceforth would be encountered in the "Con" at meetings and recitals but not on a daily basis. With the inauguration of the Conservatory Summer School program in 1937, Guerrero appeared among the available faculty, though for at least part of that summer he was in Europe. In 1938 he and Boris Berlin shared the course offerings directed to the teaching of TCM syllabus repertoire, Berlin lecturing one hour daily on the repertoire for Grades 1 through 8, and Guerrero one hour daily on that for Grades 9 and 10 and the Associateship diploma level. In a photo taken at the 1938 garden party, he appears in the far left corner, a polite but rather reluctant participant. (Was he deliberately casting himself as a shadow?) The following year he was listed in the Summer School prospectus as available for private lessons but Viggo Kihl was to give the daily lectures on "advanced" repertoire. Guerrero remained on the summer teaching list until 1944, but others (Norman Wilks, Lubka Kolessa) undertook the lectures.[34] Except for reasons of financial need, Guerrero was never enthusiastic about maintaining a teaching schedule in the city during the hot summer months, and often felt uncomfortable in formal lecture situations.

Performances

The late 1920s and the decade of the 1930s constitute the most active period of performing in Guerrero's life. He repeatedly took part in chamber music concerts, especially at Hart House and at the TCM; he appeared as soloist with the Toronto Symphony Orchestra in several seasons, and with the summer Promenade Concerts at Varsity Arena; he participated in solo and group programs in the city's brand new concert venue, Eaton Auditorium (opened 26 March 1931); he was a member of the highly successful and popular Five Piano Ensemble; and with the help of friends he undertook a remarkable cycle of intimate solo concerts devoted to rare music both old and new. Though many capable classical pianists worked in Toronto at the time, none seems to have been as versatile or as constantly in demand.

His programs with the Toronto Conservatory Trio were sometimes given in the TCM Concert Hall and sometimes in the Hart House Sunday series. A performance of the Schubert B flat Trio, 19 January 1928, formed part of a special concert marking the centenary of the composer's death. With the Conservatory String Quartet, Guerrero performed in these years both standard works for piano and strings—the Brahms Quintet in f (10 December 1928 and again 14 February 1935) and the Schumann Quintet in E flat (22 April 1930)—and lesser-known new works such as the Quintet by the French modernist Jean Cras (12 April 1934). Through Leo Smith's interest in the university's viol collection, the quartet devoted a Hart House evening to early string music, for which Guerrero prepared a group of harpsichord solos by Couperin and Rameau (13 March 1938). For probably the only occasion when he performed publicly on an instrument other than the piano, the harpsichord was a two-manual Pleyel, then

Alberto Guerrero in the late 1920s, photographed by Charles Aylett (TCM papers. Guerrero file, University of Toronto Archives)

owned by the Eaton Company but later acquired by the university music faculty. In a Hart House appearance on 20 November 1928 he played Chopin's Sonata for cello and piano in g, Opus 65, with the cellist Hans Kindler, who later gained renown as conductor of the National Symphony Orchestra, Washington. (Surprisingly, given Guerrero's familiarity both with Chopin's music and with the literature for piano and cello, this is his only known performance of the sonata.) The violinist Harold Sumberg partnered Guerrero in two duo concerts at the TCM on 28 November 1931 and 1 April 1933—congenial occasions heralding a number of later collaborations. The first concert was an all-Mozart program of four sonatas (K.305 in A, 378 in B flat, 306 in D, and 454 in B flat) and the second included sonatas by four different composers (J.S. Bach's in G, no. 6; Mozart's in E flat, K. 380; Tartini's in e; and Debussy's), ending with the *Suite italienne* arranged by Stravinsky from his *Pulcinella* ballet.

For Guerrero's first solo appearance with the Toronto Symphony Orchestra during MacMillan's régime as conductor (12 January 1932), the work was Manuel de Falla's *Noches en los jardines de España*. His solo repertoire at this time contained works by Albéniz, Granados, and Falla, and by the early keyboardists of Spain. Although this, rather than his origin in a Spanish-speaking part of the world, would have suited him to the assignment, commentators stressed that his affinity for the piece was related to his "blood." This represented for Guerrero the sort of facile assumption he never liked to make, whether about himself or other performers. He disliked the idea, for example, that only Poles could *really* play Chopin's music as it should be played, and used the example of Pablo Casals to refute the notion that only Germans *really* understood how to play Bach. His next solo vehicle with the TSO was a quite different sort of work, the massive Concerto no. 2 in B flat by Brahms, which he seems to have suggested. The performance (19 February 1935) made a formidable impression, and more than ten years later hearers were still recalling it as a highlight of their concert-going in Toronto.[35]

For the TSO's first performance of Stravinsky's *Petrushka Suite* (20 February 1934), Guerrero was called on for the demanding keyboard part: the work was originally conceived as a piano concerto. He performed the piece a second time with the orchestra in the 1935–36 season (12 November 1935). When Stravinsky appeared as guest conductor (5 January 1937), *Petrushka* was again on the program, and Guerrero was again the pianist. He spoke in later years of his pleasant brief association with the composer, who, he recalled, appreciated Guerrero as someone well acquainted with his music. Guerrero was naturally happy and animated over this experience. His daughter, then an art student in Belgium, sent him a copy of the piano arrangement of Stravinsky's *Jeu de cartes* ballet, composed just the previous year, with the inscription in English: "To Daddy, with the wish that one day I too will collaborate with him."[36] Guerrero had performed Stravinsky's Piano Sonata on several occasions and, in two Eaton Auditorium appearances in 1932, his solo contributions included the suite of pieces from *Petrushka* arranged by Stravinsky for the pianist Arthur Rubinstein, a difficult and showy score in which Guerrero is remembered to have made a brilliant impression.[37] So Stravinsky's point was accurate, that here was a musician who had more than passing knowledge of his work.

Summer orchestral concerts by Toronto Symphony Orchestra members took place in Eaton Auditorium in the first few years of that new hall, but starting in 1934 the conductor Reginald Stewart organized a popular weekly series in Varsity Arena under the name Promenade Symphony Concerts, which became firmly established, often attracting crowds of over 5,000. Guerrero appeared as soloist in the Grieg Concerto in a on 11 October 1934, and again in the same work four seasons later (4 August 1938).

Guerrero's performing repertoire continued to expand. The unexpected foray into the eighteenth-century classics, seen in the early 1920s, was followed by wider explorations, especially of J.S. Bach's clavier works.

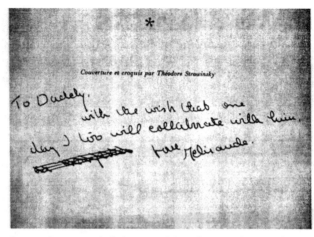

Couverture et croquis par Théodore Strawinsky

Mélisande Guerrero's autograph dedication of the gift score of Stravinsky's *Jeu de cartes*, 1937 (Collection David Finch)

He once recalled having spent an entire month, during his summer course in Saskatoon in 1931, practising one two-page Bach piece every day—the Invention no. 1 in C. He found it a wonderful microcosm of Western procedures in music, and eventually gave recitals of the whole cycle of Inventions and Sinfonias—at a time when these pieces were not regarded on the same artistic level as the larger Bach keyboard works. Guerrero gradually added all the mature Debussy piano works to his programs except the Études. *L'isle joyeuse, Jardins sous la pluie,* and *Soirée dans Grenade* had been among his basic repertoire items since he began playing publicly in Chile, and several of the Préludes (hardly known in those years) became later favourites that he repeated many times—especially *Feux d'artifice,* a new signature number, which he thought clever rather than profound, but which he played with memorable *élan,* savouring its final echoes of the *Marseillaise.* For an "all-modern" program in 1932 in Eaton Auditorium, which he shared with the Conservatory String Quartet, his group consisted of works by Debussy plus the Stravinsky suite from *Petrushka;* the quartet offered the Debussy Quartet in g and works by Casella and Bloch. For his solo concert in the same hall on 12 December the same year, Guerrero's program included two sonatas by Mozart (K.282 in E flat and K. 576 in D), Schumann's *Carnaval,* Francis Poulenc's *Mouvements perpétuels,* and again the *Petrushka* suite. Mozart and Haydn sonatas were another new direction for him, seldom evident in Chile. He seems to have lapped up the music of Poulenc and the other composers of the "Les Six" group in France as it appeared. Solo piano music by local Canadian composers is conspicuously absent, but with Blachford and Smith he played Healey Willan's Trio in b on 2 March 1927.

Guerrero had by this time established a special status with Toronto audiences. The editor of *Saturday Night,* B.K. Sandwell, commenting on the Eaton Auditorium solo recital, noted the "intense intellectual clarity" and "impeccable technique" of Guerrero's playing: "His power of selective sustaining of special notes out of a large chord is uncanny, and he can make the second note in a diminuendo sound as if he were merely changing the pitch of the first one, and not striking a fresh string." Guerrero, Sandwell said, "is not only one of the most satisfying executants in Canada but in regard to the modern French school of composition stands well up among the great concert pianists of the world."[38]

four

The Andison Concerts; Malloney's

Between 1933 and 1938, Guerrero presented a remarkable succession of solo recitals before a select subscription audience, first in the home of Gordon and Mabelle Andison, 596 Huron Street, and later at Malloney's Galleries. Andison was a professor of French at the University of Toronto, and lived in a large three-storey house in the central Annex district, within walking distance of the university. The galleries were located on the south side of Grenville Street, near Bay Street, just a few steps south of Guerrero's apartment building. Begun as a privately operated art gallery, Malloney's reopened after World War II as a cocktail lounge, still under the same name, and lasted in that form until its closing in the mid-1980s. (The Public Archives of Ontario now occupies the site.)

The programs that have survived from the series indicate Guerrero's wide-ranging interests and curiosity as a performer, and his characteristic wish to share his discoveries with like-minded intelligent listeners. As with the semi-private salon ventures depicted in the origins of the Chilean movements of his youth—the Academia Ortiz de Zárate and the Sociedad Bach in particular—the aim seems to have been cultural enlightenment rather than personal or commercial gain. Historically, the Andison and Malloney's programs have come to be regarded as important and memorable landmarks in Toronto's musical annals. The critic Christopher Wood called the series "one of the most important events in the musical life of Toronto. Other concerts may have had a wider cultural influence, but none more profound."[1] Recalling the venture years later, Andison wrote:

For me and for others who knew him well, Guerrero was Mr. XVIII century, if I might say so. His knowledge of Bach was remarkable, the ornamentation in particular....So it is no wonder that those who came to hear him at my home (8–10 recitals spread over about three years) wanted to hear the earlier music.

Although I could describe in considerable detail the genesis and general economy of these recitals given in my home (it was my wife Mabelle who was the driving force behind them)....I admit to a sketchy memory of particular programmes....

I can remember one recital devoted almost entirely to D. Scarlatti and Padre Soler. We heard a lot of 18th century music, including of course a lot of the less often heard works of Bach: French suites, Inventions, Partitas (nos. 1, 2, and 4, if my memory serves me right). There must have been one or two recitals of *modern* music, for I remember his performance of Stravinsky's Sonata.[2]

The recitals may have been initiated before the end of 1932, but the first definite date established is 6 May 1933. For that and subsequent known events, program details are as follows:[3]

6 May 1933

Galuppi	Sonata in A
Paradies	Sonata in E
Pescetti	Moderato
Soler	Two Sonatas
Mozart	Sonata in B flat, K. 333
	Sonata in D, K. 576

28 October 1933

J.S. Bach	The Well-Tempered Clavier, volume I: Preludes and Fugues nos. 1–11
	Partita no. 1 in B flat
	Chromatic Fantasia and Fugue

2 December 1933

C.P.E. Bach	Two Sonatas
Haydn	Variations [in f?]
	Two Sonatas

16 (?) December 1933

"Old Spanish sonatas, then works by Albeniz, and encores by Debussy, and Scarlatti."[4]

20 January 1934

Scarlatti	Six Sonatas
Debussy	Préludes, book 1: *Danseuses de Delphes; Voiles; Le vent dans la plaine; Des pas sur la neige; La sérénade interrompue*

Préludes, book 2: *Brouillards; La puerta del Vino; Feux d'artifice*
Jardins sous la pluie
Soirée dans Grenade
Poissons d'or
L'isle joyeuse

24 February 1934

Soler	Five Sonatas
Anglés	Aria and fugato
Gallès	Sonata in B flat
Cantallos	Sonata in c
Albéniz	*El puerto*
	Serenata
	Triana
Falla	*Andaluza*

3(?) November 1934

J.S. Bach	Partita no. 4 in D
	English Suite (no. ?)
	Italian Concerto

8(?) December 1934

Haydn	Sonata
Scarlatti	Five sonatas
Beethoven	Sonata; Variations
Mozart	Sonata[5]

30 March 1935

Soler	Three Sonatas
Cantallos	Sonata in c
Anglés	Aria and fugato
Soler	Sonata in g
Scarlatti	Two Sonatas
Satie	*Gnossienne no. 1*
	Gymnopédie no. 3
	Airs à faire fuir
Hindemith	*Kleine Klaviermusik*
Casella	*11 pezzi infantili*
Shebalin	Sonatina
Polovinkin	*Electrificat*
Villa-Lobos	*Saudades das selvas brasilieras*

23 November 1935

| J.S. Bach | Fifteen Inventions and Fifteen Sinfonias |

25 January 1936

C.P.E. Bach	Sonata in A
	Sonata in F
Haydn	Sonata in E flat (no. 52?)
	Sonata in e
Mozart	Sonata in a, K. 310

31 March 1937

"Works by Padre Antonio Soler, François Couperin, and Domenico Scarlatti."[6]

8(?) May 1937

Mozart	Sonata in G, K. 283
	Sonata in a, K. 310
	Sonata in D, (K. 311?)
Chopin	Ballade no. 1 in g
	Nocturne in F sharp
Debussy	*Reflets dans l'eau*
	Poissons d'or
	Feux d'artifice

All recitals were at the Andisons' home in 1932–33, '33–34, and '34–35, and the move to the Malloney Galleries came in the fall of 1935. Recitals began at 9:00 p.m. That the programs constituted a "subscription series" is confirmed by, among other evidence, Robert Finch's correspondence for 1933–35, a period when he was in close contact with Guerrero; these papers provide not only program details but also valuable personal comments.[7] On 17 December 1933, Finch notes that there had been ninety in the audience for the previous recital—more than the intimate space of an Annex drawing room would suggest, and more than events in public halls sometimes attract. Relations between the Andisons as hosts, Guerrero as performer, and the audience of aficionados are depicted in the notice at the bottom of the one-page typewritten program for the recital of 20 January 1934:

> NOTE: As there have been many requests to have another series of recitals next year, we should like to have an approximate idea of how many would be interested in subscribing again. The programmes this year are not only enjoyable, but of unusual interest, affording as they do the opportunity of hearing music not generally presented on the concert stage. Before requesting Mr. Guerrero to continue the preparation of further programmes, it is necessary to have at least a minimum number of subscribers, as a guarantee to him. Would you, therefore, kindly consider whether or not you would care to subscribe for next year, and also be ready to give any suggestions you might have with regard to the num-

ber and content of the programmes. If the series is repeated, we may safely assert that it will contain at least one whole programme devoted to the works of J.S. Bach.[8]

The thirteen programs cited are representative but not exhaustive. They do not include, for example, the Bach Partita no. 2 or the Stravinsky Sonata, recalled by Andison, or the *Kleine Klavierstücke,* Opus 19, of Schoenberg, which others have remembered. There is evidence that there were further programs at Malloney's, among them a trial run of Bach's *Goldberg Variations,* which Guerrero performed at the TCM Concert Hall on 11 February 1937. Harking back to the lecture on "Les Six," given for the Alliance française by Robert Finch on 1 March 1930, for which Guerrero performed a program of musical illustrations—music by Erik Satie and the six composers of the famous avant-garde group: Poulenc, Milhaud, Honegger, Tailleferre, Durey, and Auric—it seems likely that he revived this program for his Huron Street or Grenville Street followers.

The repertoire by the early Iberian keyboardists had only recently become widely available through the volumes published in France under the editorship of Joaquin Nin.[9] Guerrero was among the first to specialize in this music by the inheritors of Domenico Scarlatti in eighteenth-century Portugal and Spain. To illustrate the music of Soviet Russian composers, Guerrero chose two lesser names instead of the more widely known Prokofiev and Shostakovich: the suggestions and indeed the scores may have come from his friend Boris Berlin, who maintained musical contacts with the USSR. In presenting the entire Bach Inventions and Sinfonias, Guerrero arranged them in pairs, Invention no. 1 followed by Sinfonia no. 1, etc., rather than playing all fifteen two-part pieces followed by all fifteen three-part ones.[10] The group of Preludes and Fugues—the first eleven of Book One—may indicate an intended performance of the entire "Forty-eight"; if this was completed, the programs have so far not come to light.

To a critic who once called Guerrero's programming of Rachmaninov a descent into doubtful taste, Guerrero responded somewhat snappily that that was the repertoire, and if you were to be a complete pianist you had to play it—it was not a question of liking it or not liking it. Part of being a complete pianist, his example seems to indicate, also included neglected old and new reaches of the repertoire, lovingly presented to small coterie audiences.

The series was not reviewed in the daily press, but several concerts received notices in the weekend publication *Saturday Night* by such writers as Reid MacCallum, Marcus Adeney, Raymond Mullens, Christopher Wood, and the young Northrop Frye. The detailed comments often appear to reflect the intimate atmosphere of the concerts. "He plays the notes [in Bach] just as they were written and plays them with very little pedal but with an astonishing variety of touch" (Mullens). "The reading of the ornaments was careful and authoritative" (Frye). "Delectable performances. The particular, almost brittle, touch which Mr. Guerrero has developed for the music of [Mozart's] period makes for great clarity of outline and for an unsentimental coolness of expression which is never merely dull or devoid of life" (Wood).[11]

Friendships

The move to Grosvenor Street and the growing permanence of his life with Myrtle Rose marked also the development of a close circle of friends that was to last to the end of Guerrero's life. Rather than professional musicians, its members were mainly University of Toronto academics— Norman Endicott of the University College English department and his wife Betty, a librarian; Robert Finch and Gordon Andison, both of the University College French department, and Andison's wife, Mabelle; Laure Rièse of the Victoria College French department; Reid MacCallum of the Department of Philosophy and his wife Alice, an amateur violinist. To these were sometimes added a non-academic couple, Lieutenant Colonel William R. Patterson and his francophone wife who, as "Madame Pat," was well known in musical circles as a teacher of French language and diction. Especially with the Endicotts, Finch, and the Andisons, Guerrero formed the habit of regular (often weekly) intimate dinners. There were discussions about literature, art, and music, and occasionally musical performances, either live, or (notably often) via the radio or the phonograph: Andison and Finch were both capable pianists, and they and other members of the group were avid record collectors, as were Guerrero and Rose.

Robert Finch (1900–95) left a lively record of this social circle. A noted polymath, best known as a distinguished poet but active also as a painter, pianist, stage actor, and scholar of French literature, Finch came to Guerrero for piano lessons in 1933–34. His account is found in a diary-like succession of entries forming several lengthy typed instalment-letters, of which he kept carbon copies.[12] The letters, some of them forty pages long, are addressed to "Dear Ian," identified as Isaac Pearson, later known as Ian Mackinnon-Pearson, a Canadian business executive and art connoisseur living in Paris. On his summer leaves in the mid-1930s, Finch made the home of Pearson and his wife Cecilia Mackinnon his French headquarters. The following quotations from this remarkable quasi-journal reflect on Guerrero and his friends at this period:

6 November 1933: "G's friend Myrtle (who is always at his side now)…."

9 November 1933: "Andison told me he was going to play the D minor concerto next Sat. week, with the little string orch. one of Guerrero's pupils runs.…'And you are going to play with them some time, aren't you?' he asked. 'No doubt,' I said. The fact is Guerrero has never mentioned it to me. And I am not going to press him."

10 November 1933: "At 6 o'clock I…went over to Guerrero's where he was offering cocktails to the Andisons who were going to offer him dinner at their house to follow, all this in celebration of some very vague event…I was surprised that G would have cocktails, for he thinks them bad for the stomach."

11 November 1933: "Guerrero was just finishing with…Jack Samaloff, on the G maj. Concerto of Mozart. Then I had mine on a new Haydn sonata, Toccata by Poulenc; am to do the Haydn again; G thinks the P doesn't suit me…[Later:]…then went back to G's for dinner, as usual on Sat. night. Myrtle Rose was there, prepared the dinner, very good…Just as we were finishing the Andisons appeared, to my intense surprise, for our Sat. nights had usually been quite quiet. They had come to listen to something on the radio, but it broke just as G turned it on, so we had to talk." [Later (12 Nov), Guerrero tells Finch how put out Mrs Andison was about this; it spoiled her evening]: "'Aren't women impossible,' he said."

13 November 1933: [Guerrero comments on the healthy appearance of Edward ("Weedy") Magee, "an ex-pupil of Guerrero's"]: "There's a reason…: He and his wife have gone to live with *her* parents, so they have no more drinks." "A few minutes later we were at the Gov't Vendor's, G wishing to get bottle of wine (St. Julien) and there was—emerging from the front door—Weedy." [Later, to Andison's, to hear his reading of Mozart's Concerto in d, K.466]: "[Louis?] Murch, G's pupil, energetically conducting."[13]

2 December 1933: [Guerrero] "not well, and dreading this evening's recital, second in the series of four chez les Andison.…We ran over the programme together…Finally I brought him home to lunch, for I discovered he was going to mould off to Eaton's, Myrtle having gone to hear 'Butterfly.' (We are having a week of opera here).…We found that his Mozart middle movement was very different from my edition…I went to dinner at the Endicotts afterward, and then on to the recital with them. The house was packed this time. The program went well I thought, the tempi being splendid, there was none of that hard brilliance that had shown in the Mozart he played last year."[14]

3 December 1933: "After lunch went to G's to hear radio symphony pro-gramme from N.Y. [outline of program]....Went back home to tea. Then returned to G's where I wished to discuss something in connection with the series of talks on defining one's attitude to music, but the Andisons arriv-ing, I took my departure."

9 December 1933: "Went immediately to Guerrero's for the massage.[15] Then home, and worked until time for my music lesson at 4, which I took in G's flat, as he is still weak with his cold. Very successful, a Haydn sonata. He came to dinner with us here, as Myrtle was going out, and he did not feel up to cooking." [Later the same evening, G plays in a benefit concert at Massey Hall], "in aid of unemployed musicians." [Outline of mixed program: band, choir.] "Guerrero played well, two selections, and was recalled several times. On the whole [the concert] was amusing and pathetic combined."[16]

17 December 1933: [Finch mentions a portrait sketch of Guerrero he is working on].[17]

[n.d., evidently a continuation]: "G took me in the taxi he had got for himself and Myrtle. When we got out I ran round to the Endicotts, who had asked me to look in first...Norman [Endicott] was chafing already to go to the recital. Betty had a cold and thought better to stay in. The night was bit-ter. We raced round the corner to the Andisons. About ninety people came to this last recital of the series. (Spanish music.) I sat first beside [Reid] McCallum...Meredith Glassco had come with Mme. P[atterson]. Also a Mr Gianelli."

23 December 1933: "To Guerrero's for dinner. Cooked by Myrtle... [menu]...Barsac for wine. We had been going to play some music, a little celebration but a musician, a Mr. Wilks, came in, and he is conversational, reminiscent....We did play a little, inventing some, then doing pieces G has written for children."[18]

6 January 1934: "I had supper with Guerrero and Myrtle. We talked about French books and then about Spanish poetry. I am making some translations from the latter with G's help."

24 February 1934: "Tuesday eve. I went to the Toronto Symphony Orches-tra chiefly to hear Guerrero do the piano part of Pétrouchka. I went with Miss Rose (Myrtle) and sat in the fifth row....Myrtle and I went back-stage to get G but the Andisons and Mme. P. were already there, so we dis-creetly faded out and went home. We had both wanted G to get home to bed early, as he is to play the last recital of his series (at the Andisons' home) this Saturday evening.—Myrtle tells me Mrs. Andison would like to

leave the friends she is living with, and take an apartment with Guerrero. And but for the arrangement Myrtle has with G (cooking for him in return for lessons) Mrs. A would undoubtedly go ahead with the idea. When Myrtle told her she was going to Philadelphia for a few days in connection with some musical venture or other (conference, I think) Mrs A exclaimed spontaneously: 'Oh, you might get a job there!'"

25 November 1934: [Discussion concerning a recent Bach concert by Harold Samuel.][19] "'Oh, but there is no "way" to play Bach,' said Mrs. H, 'he didn't leave any directions as to how to interpret his music, so there are as many ways of playing it as you like.'[20] I was horrified to hear this remark. On telling Guerrero he said, 'But Bach did leave directions as to how to play his music. He left the notes themselves on the page, and each note has its definite value. And that is precisely the first instruction of Bach's that Harold Samuel neglected.'—I thought this a very sound remark. Guerrero…said that only two notes in the whole program received a perfectly true as-written value…(But imagine that anyway at the piano after Wanda [Landowska] au clavecin!) (I couldn't go to the Samuel because of my evening class.)"…"On Saturday the 17th I took a lesson on the sonatas of J. Christian Bach in order to illustrate Lady Windle's lecture, to be given on the 27th." [Evidently no regular weekly lessons now.]

[n.d.]: [Account of the first meeting of the Mozart Society] "held at the Women's Art Rooms. The meeting was held in the afternoon, mostly women of middle-age were present.…When Guerrero had played his sonatas, the president…thanked him saying: 'It seems to [me] incredible that a Spanish gentleman should be able to do such justice to German music.' He was about to inform her politely that he was from Chile, and that in any case his origin had nothing to do with the music, but desisted.…At the close of the meeting, the one who is prime mover in the new society [?] came up to him and said: 'Thanks so much, Mr. Guerrero, I'm of course glad we have a Mozart Society here now, but I cannot help thinking that my poor dear husband would have preferred it to be a Beethoven one.'"

[29 November 1934]: [Group gathers to hear Wanda Landowska's recording of Bach's *Goldberg Variations*] "chez Guerrero. Davis [?] and his wife came (with their set of the discs), Douglas D[uncan], Norman Endicott, Roy Daniells, Victor Lange, Myrtle Rose, and a student of mine, Alan Jarvis.[21] The records sounded perfect…Davis is leaving his records with Guerrero who is going to put them in 'form' by playing them with his Burmese needles a few times, and on his more powerful machine. After the Goldberg G put on the Strawinsky Octuor which contains a set of variations, and thus makes an extremely interesting contrast."

[date unclear]: "Tuesday: in evening to recital given by Myrtle Rose's children from public schools. These are just ordinary children, but all showed the benefit of splendid teaching. All the pieces had been specially written by Guerrero, and carefully graded, containing only intervals of real value, not aiming at originality but at purity. No names are given the pieces...so as not to induce wrong associations in the children's minds, but they are allowed to name their own pieces if they like. The names so given die automatically when taken up by a new pupil." [Friday:] "[Andison] complains to Guerrero that the great fault of our lecturers here is their anxiety to convey information. Gilson makes you enjoy the hour or two, without loading you up with information.[22] 'Be careful' Guerrero informed him 'after taking out the information, you may find you have nothing left.'"

16 December 1934: [Comments on recital by Moiseiwitsch, program of Schumann and Brahms] "Guerrero said later that certain sets of nerves were so definitely put in motion by Benno [Moiseiwitsch], that they went on operating to the detriment of technique requiring quite different sets....Wonderful virtuosity with little taste."

3 February 1935: "Friday night Guerrero played at the Alliance Française annual concert: he gave a program of modern French music, and at the end I played several 4 hand pieces with him." [program: works by Franck, Debussy, Ravel, Poulenc, Fauré, and Schmitt]

Easter Sunday, 1935: [Lengthy comments on Landowska's Couperin recordings.] "Guerrero...complained that there was not enough *bass* on the smaller machine (which I could not agree with). I wish he could hear Wanda in the flesh just *once*."

These spontaneously recorded impressions have several enlightening aspects. They offer glimpses of Guerrero's social and personal life and illustrate the interaction of personalities among his group of friends. They portray his continuing predilection for French culture. They provide a background to the Andison house concerts. In particular, they reflect the work on which Myrtle Rose was then concentrating, which would eventually lead to her collaboration with Guerrero on the two-volume *New Approach to the Piano*.[23]

Finch's naïveté regarding Guerrero's relationship with Rose may have been a pose. His evident discomfort with both Andisons probably explains the occasional gossipy aside; the rumoured crush on the part of Mabelle Andison towards Guerrero is undoubtedly a fabrication. Finch attended Wanda Landowska's summer concerts in France starting in 1933, and, an ardent devotee, clearly urged Guerrero to try and make that pilgrimage also.

Guerrero needed little persuading. Accounts of his visits to France during the 1920s are indirect; it seems there was at least one. In an interview of 1931 we read of his "having spent the greatest part of his life in South America, with the exception of a few trips to Paris"—a hint that there may have been others. His francophilia was well-acknowledged: "When asked in which country he would prefer to live, Mr Guerrero points unhesitatingly to France....Nevertheless, this talented musician likes Canada and would not return to South America to live."[24] Guerrero did spend time in Europe (mainly Paris) in the summers of 1935, '36, and '37, and visited Saint-Leu-la-Forêt, Landowska's headquarters, at least once. Myrtle Rose enrolled in Landowska's summer course in 1937. (A shipboard photo taken by Rose and remembered by several associates shows Guerrero with their friend and TCM colleague, Boris Berlin, *en route* to France. Berlin continued to Russia where he had professional and family contacts.)

The *New Approach to the Piano* represents an original view on teaching piano beginners. It seems to have been a truly collaborative effort, with Guerrero providing the creative materials in a series of little pieces and arrangements and Rose offering the results of her trial-and-error experience with teaching young players. The hand-lettered cover design for the two volumes, and the faintly *dix-huitième* tone of the subtitle, may derive from Robert Finch's interest in the project. Beginning pupils learn to read intervals on one-, two-, and three-line staves without clefs. The inclusion of rules for group participation indicates that both authors favoured class teaching of pianists (the subtitle draws attention to this, and Guerrero's earlier comments about pedagogy recommend it). There are thirty-five pieces in Book 1, ranging from one to three staves in length. Book 2 contains eighteen longer pieces, five of them duets. Most of the compositions are identified only by a number, although a few have titles such as "Conversation" or "Music Box."

The little pieces for the *New Approach,* though slight, together constitute the most original compositional effort of Guerrero's Canadian years. (As noted earlier, around the time of his emigration from Chile in 1918 he seems to have given up serious composing, even though he continued to play his own piano works in recitals.) Two short published pieces, both dated 1937, are decent and innocuous but a far cry from the challenging harmonies and forms of, say, the *Vals triste.* The Tango in D was introduced on Guerrero's recital program of 26 April 1921. He used to play it from memory, often as an encore or by request at parties, until, by his own account, the publisher Frederick Harris persuaded him to write it down. As published by Harris in 1937, it became a favourite of young pianists in Canada. Harris also made the piece available, score and parts, in orches-

BY MYRTLE ROSE AND ALBERTO GUERRERO
THE NEW APPROACH TO THE PIANO
OR HOW TO TEACH BEGINNERS
IN A MANNER BOTH AGREEABLE
AND INSTRUCTIVE, INDIVIDUALLY
AS WELL AS IN GROUPS, AND
CONTAINING   NOT ONLY
THE FIRST PART PIECES TO
BE USED IN   1   TEACHING
BUT ALSO HOW TO TEACH THEM
PUBLISHED BY THE FREDERICK HARRIS COMPANY

Cover design, *The New Approach to the Piano* by Myrtle Rose and Alberto Guerrero, 2 vols., Oakville, ON: Frederick Harris, 1935-36 (Faculty of Music library, University of Toronto)

tral versions he had commissioned from Adolf Schmid, a New York arranger—one for full orchestra and the other for a smaller theatre (or perhaps radio-studio) ensemble. The second small composition, *Southern Seas,* is a "petite valse" dedicated "to my young friends." A conventional and well-behaved waltz in D of thirty-two bars; a trio in G of the same length; a reprise of the original waltz: pleasant and easy to play and to listen to, its significance lies in the field of piano instruction, rather than that of composition.[25]

At the TCM on 11 February 1937 Guerrero performed J.S. Bach's *Goldberg Variations*, a work that at the time was a rarity known, if at all, only from recordings. It was likely through Wanda Landowska's recorded version, referred to in the Finch quotations above, that he was stimulated to master the intricacies of the two-manual harpsichord score on the piano. Ernest MacMillan, well-known as a Bach specialist, regarded it as "a monkey puzzle." Guerrero's presentation divided the Variations into three groups: the Aria-theme and nos. 1 through 11; nos. 12 through 20; and nos. 21 through 30, followed by the reprise of the Aria. Though he may have introduced the *Goldbergs* in one of his evenings at Malloney's, the work is curiously not represented in his Hart House Sunday appearances, and there is no evidence of a radio broadcast. This serious venture predates the publication of Ralph Kirkpatrick's edition, with which Guerrero however became familiar on its appearance in 1938.

"A Great Piano Town": The Five Piano Ensemble

The Swiss-born pianist and teacher Pierre Souvairan, a leading figure in the Toronto musical scene starting in the mid-1950s, used to say that the city as he found it when he arrived was "a great piano town." Before, during, and after World War II, Toronto offered a notable roster of senior piano instructors. At the TCM, along with Guerrero, were Margaret Miller Brown, B. Hayunga Carman, Reginald Godden, Viggo Kihl, Weldon Kilburn, Lubka Kolessa, Ernest Seitz, and Paul Wells—Mona Bates ran a highly successful independent studio. All had distinguished credentials and produced outstanding pupils; several (particularly Godden, Kolessa, and Seitz) were, like Guerrero, active on the concert stage and in broadcasting. Pianists outnumbered other instrumentalists several times over in conservatory enrolments, and the city's reputation as a centre of piano manufacture, while starting to decline in favour of the radio and the phonograph, was still formidable (Heintzman and Mason & Risch, the two major firms, lasted into the early 1950s). The leading international piano soloists all included Toronto in their tour itineraries (Vladimir Horowitz made virtually annual appearances in Massey Hall during my student years, for example).

A curious phenomenon was the popularity of multiple piano concerts. Piano duo teams were of course common, not just in Toronto, with their arrangements from all areas of music literature. But how many cities in that era managed to cultivate both a Five Piano Ensemble and a Ten Piano Ensemble? Guerrero's long-time association with the former, in a period when he was also mounting intimate performances of off-beat solo repertoire, is a striking parallel to his emphasis on zarzuela composition simultaneously with his groundbreaking new-music efforts in Chile years before: producing music for wide popular appeal and for connoisseurs did not represent an either-or choice for him; both were desirable and important.

The Five Piano Ensemble made its inaugural appearance in 1926, and lasted until at least 1940. The Ten Piano group came into existence in 1931 under Mona Bates's direction, seemingly as a rival effort. Both teams had strong support from Toronto piano dealers, the former from Heintzman and Company and the latter from the T. Eaton Company, local representatives of Steinway and Sons. The appearance of a large assemblage of grand pianos on stage was arresting, the locales were huge (Massey Hall, Varsity Arena, and even the city's largest sports venue, Maple Leaf Gardens), and the repertoire of the Five Piano group featured spectacular arrangements of popular piano favorites such as Chopin's Polonaise in A flat, and of orchestral standbys such as Strauss's *Blue Danube* Waltz and Chabrier's *España:* it was all well calculated to help sell instruments. A

The Five Piano Ensemble, photographed in the Heintzman showroom, 195 Yonge Street, Toronto; left to right: Reginald Stewart, Alberto Guerrero, Norah Drewett de Kresz, Viggo Kihl, Ernest Seitz (*Saturday Night*, 7 May 1927)

lengthy magazine article describes one of the first concerts and includes a striking photo of the group.[26]

This event took place at Massey Hall on 27 April 1927. The performers were Norah Drewett de Kresz, Reginald Stewart, Viggo Kihl, Ernest Seitz, and Guerrero; Ernest MacMillan conducted. As became standard programming procedure, a series of arrangements was interspersed with solos by individual members. In this all-Chopin program, the arrangements included the two most popular Polonaises—in A flat, Opus 53, and in A ("Military"), Opus 40, no. 1—and Guerrero's solos were the Impromptu in F sharp, no. 2, Opus 36, and the "Black Key" Etude in G flat, Opus 10, no. 5. For a concert in the same hall on 2 November 1927, the arrangements (should one rather call them projections?) were again all of piano originals, the only quasi-exception being Paganini's *La chasse* (originally arranged—for one piano only—by Liszt); solo offerings included Rachmaninov's Prelude in g, Debussy's *Minstrels,* Chopin's Waltz in e, op. posth., and *A Mountain Brook* by the then-novel composer Cyril Scott. For Schumann's *Carnaval,* a reviewer noted, "[the five pianists] opened in unison, and also gave the closing march in majestic unison, and took turns in playing the other short sketches."[27] Later concerts were not conducted.

At Varsity Arena on 22 October 1928, Scott Malcolm and Reginald Godden replaced Kihl and Drewett, and the program included *La campanella* (Paganini-Liszt) and the Chabrier. At Massey Hall on 23 November the same year, Liszt's Hungarian Rhapsody no. 15 and the ballet music from *Rosamunde* by Schubert were the featured group numbers. After their 15 March 1929 concert, which included Wagner's *Ride of the Valkyries,* the Scherzo from Mendelssohn's *Midsummer Night's Dream* music, and Strauss's *Beautiful Blue Danube* Waltz, a reviewer stated that the ensemble "has now become an institution in Toronto, and a popular one judging by the enthusiasm of the large crowds which attend its concerts."[28] After the group's concert of 22 November the same year, the *Conservatory*

Quarterly Review noted that "the Five Piano Ensemble…has evidently come to stay," and quoted a *Globe* review of the event: "Repetitions, recalls and encores were past counting.…The synchronizing was extraordinary throughout."[29]

In Eaton Auditorium on 5 May 1932, four members of the ensemble (Guerrero, Norah Drewett, Scott Malcolm, and Viggo Kihl) joined a small string orchestra in a performance of the Vivaldi-Bach Concerto in a for four keyboards and strings; the conductor was Géza de Kresz.

The same four, joined by Godden, appeared in Maple Leaf Gardens, on 27 November 1935, with a larger component of transcriptions in their program: the *Beautiful Blue Danube* again, Chaikovski's "Waltz of the Flowers" from *The Nutcracker,* Rimsky-Korsakov's *Capriccio espagnol,* two Liszt pieces, and a five-keyboard version of Cyril Scott's arrangement of the Invention in F by J.S. Bach. As composed by Bach, this glittering little piece lasts about thirty seconds in performance; one imagines it on this occasion as the inflation of an inflation. (Less than a week previously, Guerrero had played the complete cycle of Bach's Inventions and Sinfonias in a recital at Malloney's. Somehow he managed to compartmentalize his opposing roles as Bach purist and multi-piano team member.)

The ensemble had given another concert in the Gardens on 24 April the same year, and in 1936 they were again heard twice, in Varsity Arena, the dates being 5 May and 9 November. On 5 May and 8 September 1938 they appeared at Varsity Arena, both times with the Toronto Philharmonic, the orchestra of the summer Promenade Concerts. The conductor, Reginald Stewart, was a member of the ensemble. On 5 May he led a performance of the Vivaldi-Bach Concerto in a, with his colleagues Godden, Malcolm, Seitz, and Guerrero, and then joined them in a group without orchestra (the Bach-Scott Invention in F, Liszt's arrangement of Schubert's "Hark, Hark, the Lark," and Stravinsky's "Danse infernale"). At the 8 September concert, the ensemble replaced an indisposed guest soloist on two days' notice, and offered two pianos-only groups, highlighted by the Mendelssohn Scherzo and Weber's *Invitation to the Dance.* A further concert in Massey Hall took place on 24 November 1939. For an engagement in London, Ontario, on 14 February 1940, the ensemble members were again Godden, Guerrero, Malcolm, Seitz, and Stewart, and the program included arrangements of Bach's Toccata and Fugue in d, the "Polovtzian dances" from *Prince Igor* by Borodin, and Debussy's orchestral Nocturne no. 2 (*Fêtes*). This is the latest date for which I have located documentation.

Guerrero was the one constant member of the ensemble throughout its approximately thirteen-year existence, which may indicate that he played a leadership or organizational role. The scores of the ensemble's arrangements have not so far come to light, if in fact they were ever notated. Intriguing questions remain: who was the arranger? Was the repertoire selected and arranged by some mutual process, or did Guerrero or one of the others make assignments? And was MacMillan involved at the start in arranging for the ensemble as well as conducting it? The ensemble and its brief popularity amount to an underexplored episode in the music annals of Toronto, in which Alberto Guerrero was closely involved.

The 1940s

The start of World War II brought new people into Guerrero's life. Among his students were several refugees from Nazi-occupied Europe. Oskar Morawetz, originally from Prague, was a knowledgeable young musician, gifted both as composer and as pianist. Almost immediately upon his arrival in Toronto in 1940, he began to contribute strongly to the local music scene; his compositions were introduced in concerts, and shortly after his completion of a University of Toronto doctorate he began a long association with the university's music faculty. Guerrero cherished his broad sense of classical repertoire, while Morawetz found lessons with Guerrero, and attendance at Guerrero's performances, inspiring. In 1942 Helmut Blume, originally from Berlin, began piano studies with Guerrero. Later prominent as professor and dean of music at McGill University in Montreal and as a CBC broadcast personality, he always acknowledged the musical guidance and insights he received from Guerrero. Like Morawetz, he brought Guerrero the challenge of working with a young musician whose sense of music and its repertoire was already more developed than that of most of his Canadian pupils.

Among the Canadians, one noticeable trend in the early 1940s, and continuing thereafter, was the number of students who carried his approach to the piano into teaching careers of their own, as had Magee, Rose, and a few others in the 1930s. There are prominent examples: Gwendolyn Duchemin and Alexandra McGavin joined the teaching staff of the RCM; Victor Dell and Laurence Morton gained solid reputations respectively in the Niagara Falls region and in Interlochen, Michigan; while Frederick Skitch pioneered a piano class program at the University Settlement in downtown Toronto.

The war and its aftermath signalled changes in Guerrero's family life as well. His estranged wife, Lily, and their daughter, Mélisande, boarded a ship in Belgium on 3 September 1939, filled with Chilean citizens bound for home. A month after their safe arrival in Santiago, Mélisande, now a young woman of twenty-two, reboarded the same ship and sailed back to Philadelphia, proceeding from there to join her father in Toronto. An order-in-council of the Canadian Government dated 26 December 1941 established wartime immigration clearance for both Alberto and Mélisande, "citizens of Chile, presently residing in Toronto; intended occupation—professor of music and art student, respectively."[30] She became involved in art and theatre activities, and in June 1942 married a well-known designer, Herbert Irvine. Their son Antony ("Tony") was born 1 January 1949. Lily Wilson Guerrero returned to Toronto in late 1948 and took an apartment near the Irvines, where she was to spend the rest of her life, outliving Alberto by a dozen years, though entirely out of communication with him.[31]

Guerrero had long since cut himself off from Chilean contacts, and abandoned any idea of returning to his native country, even for a visit. Margaret Sheppard recalled from her lessons of the mid-1940s that "he greatly admired his brother Doctor Daniel and was fond of the sister in the photograph he had on display in his apartment, but as to his parents and his other siblings, he never spoke of them." He did mention his sister Amelia's husband, who "visited with him in Toronto to try to persuade him to return to Chile, and gave him difficulty conversing with him in Spanish, his native tongue. Mr G laughed when he told [Sheppard], but it surprised him."[32]

Guerrero continued to appear in recitals and broadcasts. For a joint concert with the young soprano Helen Simmie at the Art Gallery of Toronto (now the Art Gallery of Ontario) on 14 February 1943, he played Chopin and Debussy; his Chopin numbers included what appears to have been his first performance of the Andante Spianato and Grand Polonaise, Opus 22. He gave solo concerts in the Hart House Sunday Evening series in 1944, 1946, and 1948. The 30 January 1944 program included Weber's Sonata Opus 24 and Humberto Allende's *Tonada*. The latter—part of a "Hispanic" group including pieces by Villa-Lobos, Granados, and Albéniz along with Guerrero's own Tango—is a rare instance of his programming music by a Chilean contemporary. At Hart House on 13 January 1946 he ended a varied program with his own transcriptions of three harpsichord pieces by François Couperin, among them the great Passacaille in b. Unlike the unabashedly pianistic transcriptions of Bach by Tausig, Liszt, or Busoni, these were acknowledged to be imitations on the piano of the harpsichord registrations Guerrero admired in the recordings of Couperin's music by Wanda Landowska. The Passacaille in particular became a special (and much-praised) item in his later programs. He once said if he had a harpsichord he would play this music on it rather than on the piano.

In 1943 he was able to enjoy personal contacts with Landowska, whose performances he had long revered, during her extended visit to Toronto. The violinist Adolph Koldofsky had discovered manuscripts of five

Mélisande Guerrero, shortly before her marriage to Herbert Irvine, 1941 (Guerrero Collection)

keyboard concertos by Carl Philip Emanuel Bach, and the CBC contracted Landowska to play them in a series of broadcast concerts with a chamber orchestra under Koldofsky's direction.[33] The studio concerts took place between 14 March and 25 April.

For her sojourn in Toronto, Herbert and Mélisande Irvine loaned Landowska their apartment. (Herbert was then serving in the armed forces away from Toronto.) As Guerrero often recalled it, the artist astonished everyone by removing all the furniture from her practice room with the exception of her harpsichord and a small stand for her metronome. He was impressed by her austere and concentrated dedication to music. But she confided to him that she wished she *liked* the C.P.E. Bach repertoire. The concerts had a surprise aftermath: Landowska was detained at the border crossing at Niagara Falls on her way back to the USA, when it appeared she was taking the Eaton Pleyel harpsichord (on which she had done her broadcasts) with her. The misunderstanding was soon sorted out. This is the same instrument on which Guerrero had played at Hart House in 1938.

Throughout the war years there were the usual late-spring examination tours for the TCM. During part of the summer in either 1944 or 1945,

Guerrero was hired to perform at a luxury hotel, the Manoir Richelieu at La Malbaie (Murray Bay), Quebec. This was an unusual working vacation for him. He found the Manoir, on the scenic north shore of the St. Lawrence River, "a most acceptable place." "The little playing I do is not much work and 'is so wonderful, they will miss it so much when they will be home....' That is what the ladies who have reached a certain age tell me."[34]

Margaret Sheppard found Guerrero the performer to be "highly nervous." He called playing in public "a high wire act....Even when using a score he was still nervous. I remember turning pages for him when he played the Schumann Concerto on radio and we were both nervous. A great team."[35] This is not a trait stressed by other people who remember him. There is so far no documentation of the Schumann broadcast that Sheppard refers to. It was likely with a CBC studio orchestra, of which there were several in Toronto in the 1940s; in a variety-program context, the work may have been reduced to a single movement. This was the case with the Saint-Saens Concerto no. 2, for which Guerrero was soloist in the McGill Street radio studio in February 1946—and for which I was his page-turner. (I was not conscious of any nervousness on *his* part.)

He knew that, as an eager music student, I was keen for involvement, so he invited me in this capacity fairly often. A Piano Quintet by Gabriel Fauré was another instance in 1946. He played it—again in a studio broadcast, this time on a private Toronto station, CKEY—with the Conservatory String Quartet, whose members in this, the ensemble's last season, were Pearl Palmason, Goldie Bell, Harold Carter, and Joyce Sands. The CBC engaged him, with Harold Sumberg, violin, and Cornelius Ysselstyn, cello, for a series of programs devoted to the complete piano trios of Mozart, and I was the turner for at least one of these: again the precise dates remain elusive; the year was probably 1947. The CBC files indicate that he played Chopin's Sonata in b, Opus 58, in the "Distinguished Artists" recital series on 26 January 1949, and this performance is a vivid memory, along with his rehearsing for it. For a prior appearance, I believe in the same series, in either 1947 or '48, he gave another vigorous and authoritative performance from the romantic repertoire—Schumann's Fantasy, Opus 17. But of this there is no mention in the files (the program guide called *CBC Times* was not yet in existence); and, as already noted, no recording of either work has emerged, though it seems incredible that none was made.

In a memorable chamber-music performance of this period (in the 1946–47 "Five O'Clocks" series in the Conservatory Concert Hall), he joined Sumberg and Ysselstyn for a Clementi trio transcribed by Casella, followed by the Piano Trio of Maurice Ravel, in what seems to have been his only performance of that major Ravel score.

Charles Peaker, organist at the largest of Toronto's Anglican churches, St. Paul's, served as acting principal of the TCM for part of the 1944–45 season. Either in that capacity or as organizer of recitals at the church, sometimes featuring an orchestra made up of TSO professionals, and concertos with invited guest soloists, he was in touch with Guerrero. (If Guerrero appeared in the recital series the vehicle was probably the *Variations symphoniques* of Franck.)[36] As he later related, at their first meeting he addressed his colleague as "Dr. Peaker," and was told, "Oh, call me Charlie." At this Guerrero was taken aback; first names, in his world, were reserved for family, close friends, and long-time associates: he wondered bemusedly, "should I have said, 'call me Al'?"

However indifferent he may have been to professional recognition and however much he habitually distanced himself from his Chilean past, in 1946 Guerrero expressed pleasure at receiving the inaugural issues of the *Revista musical chilena,* and was touched to learn, from the article of Daniel Quiroga, that his contributions to Chilean musical life, and those of his brothers, were remembered.[37] He made a short English paraphrase of this item, the pencil manuscript of which is preserved in the University of Toronto Archives.[38] He remarked at the time that Canada had no equivalent publication to the *Revista.*

five

Lessons

I had regular piano lessons with Guerrero from the fall of 1945 through the early summer of 1950. In June 1945 he heard me play in my home town of Victoria as a TCM examination candidate. I still have his exam report, a mighty example of "telling it as it is." If I had inflated ideas of my own pianistic abilities, the report points out basic inadequacies: rushed tempi, blurred trills, and a considerable catalogue of other faults. He awarded me a grade slightly under first class; while this was a disappointment, I knew it was just. At the same time, Guerrero evidently recognized a certain musical aptitude worth developing, because I soon learned he had recommended me for a scholarship to come to Toronto for full-time music study. The terms left me free to choose any teacher on the conservatory's staff, but his frank appraisal and the urging of another Victorian, Alexandra McGavin, then already in his class, led me to sign up with Guerrero.

The lessons took place in the brightly lit sunroom studio, a relaxing space of cool colours, with shelves of books and scores, large prints of Renoir and Picasso on the walls, and, on a side table, a framed invitation to the funeral of Frédéric Chopin. Years later a fellow student, Margaret Sheppard, recalled, "taking the elevator to the top floor and then walking up the stairs to the studio penthouse with its wall of windows lined with red geraniums, a print of Picasso's *Woman in White* nearby, the two baby grand pianos at one end…and over all the soft green hue that gave a Latin atmosphere to the room, even in the midst of a wicked Toronto winter."[1]

To say my lessons opened a whole new world would be understating the case. We worked towards a more relaxed and more confident technique, and I learned the various exercises Guerrero found effective to this end—

Alberto Guerrero, photographed by Allan Sangster, ca. 1937 (Collection Stuart Hamilton)

more interesting and more logical than the traditional keyboard exercises of Czerny and others. The muscular power needed for piano playing was, he showed, not enormous. Snapping a finger against a table top makes an already loud noise; much of the action required for even a strongly projectile forte need come only from the fingers. Ninety per cent of the repertoire was best presented with a solid finger technique: with the upper arm supporting the forearm and hand, the fingers were free to attack the keys. They had to play to the depth of the keys, and to stay close for accuracy. A photo of Guerrero taken in the late 1930s shows him with one hand in midair—an indication, I thought, that the shot was posed, rather than snapped in actual performance. For accuracy also, major changes of hand-position (the wide skips in Scarlatti, for example) were taken laterally—that is, sideways rather than up and down. He was critical of professional recitalists who "slapped" at the keys with the forearms, finding this an inefficient approach, besides which the impact destroyed tone. A New York reviewer of the period described a well-known pianist, Ania Dorfmann, as "swatting" the piano, and added that at one point he "could have sworn the piano swatted back": Guerrero enjoyed quoting this bit of sarcasm.[2] Swatting with the forearm was not his style, even in massive chordal passages by Chopin or Brahms or Franck: there were other, more musical ways of delivering power.

His recommended exercises were important, but mostly we pupils learned technique by facing the problems of actual repertoire. In the first years I covered major Chopin and Schumann works (Études, Preludes, Waltzes, a Ballade, a Scherzo of Chopin's, and Schumann's *Études symphoniques*); Beethoven's Sonatas in B flat, Opus 27, no. 1, and in A, Opus 101, and his Bagatelles, Opus 126; Mozart's Fantasia in c, K.475, and Sonatas in a, K.310, and D, K.311; a Brahms Rhapsody and several Intermezzi; some Bartók, some Hindemith, Milhaud's *Saudades do Brasil,* Ravel's *Valses nobles et sentimentales;* Debussy's *Jardins sous la pluie,* as well as several of the Préludes. Above all, there was always a lot of Bach: movements from the French and English suites, Preludes and Fugues from the *Well-Tempered Clavier,* and eventually the cycle of Inventions and Sinfonias. I found these amazing one- and two-pagers an absorbing study, and in lessons we would probe questions of tempo, touch, and especially ornamentation. Soon Guerrero had me comparing editions and reading the literature on style and performance practice. When I had played the cycle in public satisfactorily a few times, he suggested I should learn the *Goldberg Variations*, and to do so under his guidance was truly inspiring. It made me recognize that the source of his insistence on attention to voice-leading behaviour in *any* music—a Chopin Waltz, a Brahms Intermezzo, the inner textures of a Debussy Prélude—was Bach.

Gaining in confidence, I started playing in student recitals, in festival contests, and eventually in full concerts and broadcast recitals. Guerrero teamed me with Ray Dudley for experience in the four-hand repertoire. As a teacher, he was a steady, encouraging, and critical presence. After a public performance his backstage greeting was always upbeat: the playing was "marvellous," which is what a performer wants to hear, but at the next lesson, the analysis would be more candid. Once I took him a Brahms piece I was scheduled to play on the radio. I obviously had not practised it nearly enough, and Guerrero was scathing: did I really intend to play like that in a public broadcast? He made it as a rational comment, not in anger.

I brought Guerrero my early attempts at composition, and he took the time to consider them, encouraged me, made constructive comments, as we know he did with so many other young aspiring composers. He questioned what I regarded as my "modernism"—the somewhat forced avoidance of tonal cadences, for example—not to condemn this or other such traits as errors of taste but rather to get me to affirm that what I wrote was actually what I wanted to *hear.* He appeared happy about the direction of these compositional efforts, but impatient at times with my other varied activities—participation in student stage productions, for example, and literary involvements (program notes, publicity, concert reviews)—all of which took time away from my piano labours. At length he depicted my future not as an ambitious high-powered concertizer but as a musician whose motivations might lead in several different channels. He once said, after I had played a recital, "You could be a *very interesting* pianist." I regarded this as a tremendous compliment.

He and Myrtle Rose attended some of my acting attempts. After one of these, he was preparing for a Christmas party of his class, and asked me to get up a comic monologue for the occasion. I was reluctant; it didn't seem appropriate somehow in front of my fellow pianists. "Well," said Guerrero, "if you don't, I'm afraid they'll start to sing Christmas carols." I think of this every year when secular crowds, both public and private, are moved to blare out those much-abused nineteenth-century tunes with their weird nineteenth-century religious sentiments. For Guerrero the custom was objectionable not so much on religious grounds as by its musical crudeness and banality, or so I gathered (he did not elaborate, and he never preached).

Our discussions hardly ever touched on religion, though I got the clear impression he was an agnostic and a fatalist. He said to a member of the clergy who visited him in his last illness, "I respect Jesus the man, but I have no faith in his divinity."[3] He told William Aide, apropos of his skepticism, that once when he was examining for the RCM in a convent, one of the nuns had offered him a bribe.[4] When he noticed I was reading some Marxist literature, he said I should be asking whether there were elections in the USSR. Once Margaret Sheppard corrected him in pretended haughtiness on the spelling of her surname; he wondered, did she think it made her superior to those who spelled it "Shepherd"? A mention of some book by D.H. Lawrence elicited the only comment on sex I can recall he ever made to me. He wondered why North Americans (I think he meant WASPs) seemed to think there was something *mysterious* about sex. As always, he did not elaborate.

We spoke about comedy. At a well-mounted local performance, in English, of *The Marriage of Figaro,* a well-known society matron was overheard to say it was "just like Gilbert and Sullivan!"—missing, Guerrero thought, the poignant touches that are the deep foil to the farce. There was a revival of some of Chaplin's films, and a spate of intellectual analyses of them. Guerrero considered Chaplin's work overrated; his favourite film comedian was Raimu in *La Femme du boulanger.*

Guerrero the teacher was a disciplinarian, not a dictator. Once an administrator called from the RCM about a pupil who had just registered with him and was making slow progress. "He needs a stronger hand," he

Alberto Guerrero with his daughter's oil portrait, photographed by Margaret Sheppard, 1943 (Collection J. Beckwith)

said over the phone. "You should send him to Margaret." His colleague Margaret Miller Brown was known as a tough taskmistress. His way was not to dictate but rather to insist on honesty. "He could be as hard as nails," said one his last pupils, William Aide.[5] Music for him was no fake book. One of the few literary allusions I can recall hearing from him, and more than once, referred to the episode in *Don Quixote* where Sancho Pança tries to persuade his master that instead of doing all his mad "heroic" escapades he could just *say* he did them, who would know the difference?—to which the Don replies that such was not the tradition of the great knights of old: they *really fought* their battles.

In 2001 I was invited to contribute a short piece about Guerrero for the "Great Piano Teachers" column in the British publication *Piano*. It was an opportunity to try and capsulize the principles of not only piano playing but also musical judgment in general that I owe to my studies with him.

> Though authoritative in its command of technique, Guerrero's musicianship was distinct from that of most pianists in…its breadth of reference. During [the post-World War-II period], new translations of the performance-practice treatises of Couperin, Quantz, Leopold Mozart, Emanuel Bach, and others, started to appear. Guerrero devoured them. The amount of space they devoted to questions of ornamentation proved for him that this was an essential aspect of early keyboard music, not a superfluous extra. Distinctness of part playing (in *any* music, not just "early" kinds or polyphonic kinds) meant appreciating, for example, the re-entry of the bass after some bars of rest, or differences between high,

middle, and deep registers of the instrument. Instrumental evocations became like the small-type indications in a Messiaen score: the harpsichord could be suggested in a lightly pedalled semi-staccato, the lute or guitar in similar ways; a cantilena could borrow some of the expressive suggestions of Leopold Mozart for string music; in a passage in thirds he would ask for "more second oboe." Long notes in a varied texture called for the ringing vitality of brass or organ, somehow countervening their inevitable decay. Some rhythms were best regarded as "unbarred," like Renaissance vocal music. Reasoning that it was a survival of the unnotated double-dotting of composers such as Handel, he startled listeners by playing the first upbeat in *Carnaval* as a sixteenth, not an eighth.

...

Performance in his view needed to retain what he called a certain "earthiness." Listening to a recording by, I think, the Philadelphia Orchestra, of *L'après-midi d'un faune,* he found the opening flute solo too perfect: he wanted it rawer-sounding, more "pagan." He responded to such qualities in Teyte's singing or Segovia's guitar-playing, and would get the student to bring them out in passages such as the "big tune" in [Debussy's] *Les collines d'Anacapri.* Music was a wonderful varied territory and one needn't live on the mountain top the entire time.

...

As a teacher he had exceptional resources but no "method." A number of colleagues in the 1940s were adopting the ideas of E. Robert Schmitz. Though admiring Schmitz's playing, Guerrero was sceptical of the ideas, especially the sometimes bizarre fingering solutions; he observed that what might work for one student would not necessarily work for another. I was interested to read William Aide's recollection from his studies with Guerrero: "He dismissed, sarcastically, my attempts to scribble his comments on my scores, so I stopped."[6] I had the same experience, some years before. The comments were immediate and practical, not words of wisdom to be preserved or turned into a "method."[7]

In the years 1948 to 1950, while still taking regular lessons with Guerrero, I held a job as publicist for the Royal Conservatory, and as part of my duties I had to make up-to-date CVs of the staff. Asking Guerrero for information about his own career, I received the reply that still haunts me: "I have no story." I had started a *Monthly Bulletin,* containing mainly staff and student news but also incorporating "think-pieces" by various teachers, and I was successful in persuading Guerrero to contribute to this series. The edited typescript of his short article, "The Discrepancy between Performance and Technique," is in the University of Toronto Archives.[8] (The article is reproduced in full as Appendix 1.) Its central point, deriving from a popular study by the French writer Alexis Carrel (1873–1944), was that "the hand is part of the mind."[9] It was a novel idea in 1950, but it has since been taken for granted in neurology (not to mention computer science), that mental operations do not consist of exchanges of "messages" between the brain and the nervous system. Guerrero's celebration of the miracle of the human hand has achieved a modest circulation. He pooh-poohed the idea of preserving his thoughts, but this article makes one regret he did not write more.

Changes

During the 1940s, several changes in leadership at the Toronto Conservatory of Music introduced changes in policy and in relations between the school's administration and its parent body, the University of Toronto. Sir Ernest MacMillan relinquished the principalship in 1942, though he retained his position as dean of the University's music faculty.[10] Norman Wilks, MacMillan's deputy, took over as principal but died two years later, and, after a brief interregnum, Ettore Mazzoleni was named principal. It was Mazzoleni, a graduate of Oxford and the Royal College of Music, who initiated the move to rename the institution the Royal Conservatory of Music of Toronto, and in 1946, its diamond jubilee, George VI gave permission for the change.

In contrast to the program curtailments during the war years, the later 1940s saw a burgeoning of talent and ideas, marked in particular by the return of war veterans for advanced study. For students it was a vital and stimulating period. New programs included a conservatory "senior school" that was modelled after the advanced-level programs of the Juilliard School in New York and devoted to structured courses for professional performers. Senior performance teachers including Guerrero found their services in demand in new ways. The senior-school curriculum was devised by Arnold Walter, an Austrian-born composer and pianist who had settled in Toronto in 1938. A man of exceptional intellectual background, he had a vision for reforming music education in Toronto, and indeed in Canada at large, and in the next few years succeeded in translating many of his ideas into action. One had only to observe the trends in American universities at the time to conclude that the senior-school program would have a better chance of support as part of the university Faculty of Music (which was then itself expanding in several other directions). In an explosive manoeuvre in 1952, a sort of "palace putsch," the university established a new structure with Mazzoleni and Walter as heads respectively of the Royal Conservatory and the faculty. There was such animosity between these two leaders that, once MacMillan resigned, a fresh dean was appointed more or less as a referee; he was Boyd Neel, a newcomer from Britain.

Guerrero kept on with his routine, teaching now at the peak of his abilities, performing less often but still at a superb level. His view of the increasingly structured program for his students was skeptical. Although he appreciated the dramatic new attention it paid to professional music study, he doubted the effectiveness of classes and lectures compared to one-on-one studio sessions. When he was occasionally asked to lecture, he performed seriously and with a personal touch, but he seemed just as glad not to be asked. The increased competitiveness among teachers upset him. He found it difficult to cooperate with Arnold Walter after he discovered that Walter was offering inducements to his pupils to leave Guerrero for another teacher. They were different temperaments: Walter was a boss—a boss with imagination and vision but a boss nonetheless—while Guerrero was a master. It took a few seasons before Walter would concede Guerrero's success with several of his most brilliant students.

(There was an ironic corollary. After Guerrero's death, Walter became an international figure in music education and regularly travelled to conferences. His coach for Spanish conversation was Lily Wilson Guerrero; they became good friends.)

Guerrero's generation faced a rapid and decisive change in North American music education: composers and performers, formerly raised in conservatories, were now enrolling in university music departments.[11] While Guerrero epitomized the humanistic approach to music studies, he resisted the formation of lecture courses and the structured curricula of that approach. In his view, one gained a sense of style by studying scores and learning to play them correctly, not by reading a book or attending a series of learned talks under the title "Style." He kept abreast of the scholarly literature, subscribing to the *Musical Quarterly* and the *Revue musicale* and adding significant new publications to his personal library, but he regarded writing music and playing music as the essence of the discipline, rather than merely its "applied" aspects (a term just then coming into use in music-education circles).

By the late 1940s, Guerrero's personal situation had also changed. He became free to marry, either through Lily's eventual relaxation of her opposition, or because Ontario laws broadened to make protracted separation a new grounds for divorce. On 2 November 1948, he and Myrtle Rose were married in a civil ceremony in Toronto. In the early summer of 1949, at their Lake Simcoe cottage, a second ceremony was performed by the Very Reverend James Endicott, Norman Endicott's father.[12] Friends recognized the happiness this turn of events brought to both Myrtle and Alberto. The pair travelled to British Columbia, and leased a lovely ranch-style mountainside house in West Vancouver, overlooking the harbour. Guerrero practised Chopin all summer, particularly the exhilarating Étude in C, Opus 10, no. 1. My fiancée, Pamela Terry, and I visited them, and took photos. They came to see Pamela perform in Anouilh's *Antigone* at the University of British Columbia playhouse.

Alberto Guerrero and Myrtle Rose Guerrero, photographed by Pamela Terry, West Vancouver, August 1949 (Collection J. Beckwith)

In early 1950 it became clear Myrtle was going to have a child. She kept up her teaching schedule and was in good health and high spirits. After my Bach recital on 21 March she and Guerrero hosted one of their wonderful, generous receptions in the sunroom studio. Bearing her first child at forty-three was a brave undertaking for Myrtle Rose, and she appeared to be measuring up marvellously. In May, however, the child, Ana Maria, was born with a defective heart, and lived less than three weeks.[13] It was a devastating end to great hopes, for both prospective parents. That they rallied and continued with their lives, moving into a new phase with courage, is a tribute to both their characters. *With courage*, but without the connection to the future they had envisioned.

Glenn Gould

In a popular French-language biography of the pianist Glenn Gould, the author states, accurately, that Guerrero taught Gould from 1943 to 1952. He adds, fancifully, that Guerrero then "humbly recognized that he had nothing further to teach him."[14] This hagiographic view of Gould's talent has been common in biographies that invariably cast Guerrero in the role of the humble, if not limited, teacher. One recalls the film *A Song to Remember* in which Paul Muni, as Elsner, remarks to Cornell Wilde, as the young Chopin, "You didn't learn that from me, Frederick, you learned it from God."

The mystique surrounding Gould's miraculous career has allotted Guerrero a curious and distorted role—more or less that of a kindly, indulgent old uncle. Only in the late 1990s and early 2000s were attempts made to correct the balance: notably, William Aide's memoir *Starting from Porcupine* and the major Gould biography by Kevin Bazzana, *Wondrous Strange*, have examined the relationship fully and with due fairness.[15]

Guerrero was immensely impressed with the eleven-year-old Gould, and found his greatest challenge as a teacher to develop his genius to the full. (Gould may also have been impressed. Kevin Bazzana discovered a doodle in one of Gould's grade-school notebooks, preserved in the Gould Collection, Library and Archives Canada, Ottawa, in which a large capital "G" joins together three names: Gould, Guerrero, Greig [*sic*]. Through his mother Florence Greig, Gould was a distant relative of the Norwegian composer Edvard Grieg.) It was partly a matter of gradually opening up his pupil's musical tastes: he once said that when Gould started out he used to play the Beethoven slow movements "as if they were hymn tunes." Protestant hymn singing was indeed a fundamental part of Gould's childhood experience of music, and in the nineteenth century some Beethoven slow movements had been set to hymn texts—but Guerrero's point was to recognize the essence of the slow movement character in the classical piano-sonata context. He worked for similar recognition of the essential musical context of the stylized dances of Bach and Couperin (he got Gould to play his transcription of the Couperin Passacaille). Gould's student performances of works like Chopin's Impromptu in F sharp, no. 2, and Mendelssohn's *Variations sérieuses,* though forgotten in the pianist's professional maturity, were beautiful stepping stones towards his command of the piano. Guerrero introduced his pupil gradually to new avenues of repertoire—succeeding brilliantly with the Elizabethan virginalists and with Schoenberg, though failing to ignite the spark with the Debussy that he so valued.

But there was also the building of a technical fluency and technical assurance such as few pianists have acquired. As Margaret Sheppard put it, "It has to be obvious to anyone who is not wearing blinders that Glenn learned his technical skills from Guerrero."[16] Gould studied to sit low at the keyboard, address the keys with a low wrist and flat fingers, and support his arms from the shoulder blades—all attitudes for which Guerrero's playing style provided the model. Many students remarked that Gould's playing always reminded them of Guerrero's. Perhaps because younger observers didn't know Guerrero, they reverse this observation. For example, the Gould expert Kevin Bazzana has viewed the entire Gould video archives, and when I showed him Mélisande Irvine's oil portrait of

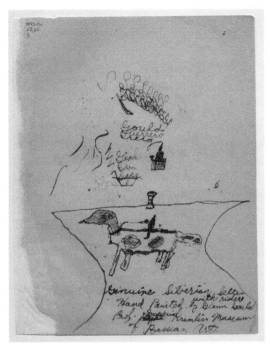

Marginal doodles in a school notebook by Glenn Gould, ca. 1943, shortly after he began studies with Alberto Guerrero (Library and Archives Canada, Ottawa, Gould Collection), reproduced courtesy of the estate of Glenn Gould.

her father at the keyboard, he immediately said "that's just like Glenn." Guerrero and Gould, both taller than average with lanky arms, had naturally a similar posture—*apostura,* as Guerrero's early critics in Chile called it. This became exaggerated the more Gould worked at the keyboard. To an interviewer who commented on his crouched-over position at the piano, Gould said, "that's the way my teacher taught me, and I can't change now. My teacher's the biggest hunchback in Canada."[17] In his sixties Guerrero had put on extra weight and become somewhat round-shouldered; this was an unkind personal remark.

Though in later years Gould claimed to practise very little, as a young pupil (and from then well into his twenties) he put in long diligent practice time. William Aide has usefully imagined what it must have been like.[18] It clearly included hours spent in Guerrero's method of "finger tapping." A series of candid photographs of Gould taken in 1956 shows him with one hand poised over the other, obviously engaged in finger-tapping a practice passage.[19] Guerrero adapted the tapping procedure from Otto Ortmann's writings on piano technique, and passed it along to all his students in those years.[20] Two of Gould's fellow pupils describe it:

> With a relaxed hand, we allowed the fingers to rest on the keys and then, with the other hand, tapped them one at a time at the tip and let them bounce back into place.[21]

> You placed one hand on the keys, with fingers over the required notes, then used a finger of the other hand to push on the first knuckle of the first hand with the pressure needed to produce the sound.[22]

The goal of this approach was, as Aide says, "absolute evenness and ease in tricky passage work." It accounts for the clarity of individual notes in Gould's fast runs, one of his most indelible personal trademarks as a player. After tapping, the next stage of mastering a passage would be to play it in a slow staccato; in the final in-tempo performance the notes were not necessarily intended to be separated in such a detached way, but Gould came to prefer that touch. That Gould mastered and used the tapping technique is verified by Ray Dudley, the pupil who was closest to Gould in student days. In an article about Guerrero's teaching and about Gould's technical formation under Guerrero, Dudley says he and Gould sometimes used to practise together the same exercises that their teacher had assigned.[23]

Guerrero convinced Gould that he could memorize a major musical work away from the keyboard, by just studying the score page by page.[24] The favourite pupil of Guerrero's last years, Pierrette LePage, describes this approach: "It was a bit late, and there wasn't much time to learn the Concerto we had chosen (Liszt E♭)—so [Guerrero] suggested that I memorize one page at a time, by reading it, like you memorize a poem, and then play it on the piano. I remember doing that on the bus, on the way home from school. In less than 3 weeks I could play the whole Concerto (from memory of course)."[25] LePage adds that she found the procedure "very stressing," and "never learned another piece that way." But for Gould, already endowed with exceptional memory powers, it became standard.

As an illustration of both musical and physiological points made by Guerrero, I found Gould's performance of the Prelude in b flat from Bach's *Well-Tempered Clavier,* Book 1, in 1946, to be a marvel: the contrapuntal give-and-take was totally convincing, just as Guerrero always asked, and the expression was powerful and gripping. Gould was then all of thirteen.

Were we other pupils envious of Gould? From observation of myself and others, I would say we never were. He was exceptional, and try as we might we would not likely acquire either his drive or his uncanny ability to compel listeners' attention. I could never play *that* well, I remember thinking at his memorable 1946 performance of the first movement of Beethoven's Fourth Concerto. That was sheer genius. But if genius entails the usually attributed proportions of inspiration and hard work, it was

Guerrero who showed the proper directions for the work and Glenn who worked.

Although I was not jealous of my friend and fellow pupil, I may have had some resentment of Guerrero's favouring him in specific situations. Two may be worth describing. One afternoon in February 1946, Glenn and I were both selected, from a preliminary Bach class of about two dozen pianists at the local competition festival, to be finalists—meaning we would repeat our performances that same evening. When I phoned to tell Guerrero this, he immediately invited me to turn pages for the Saint-Saens radio performance he was scheduled to play at around the supper hour. Of course I accepted, and of course the excitement of his playing diverted me from concentration on my own looming Bach. As a result, I played considerably less well than I had earlier in the day. Had Guerrero manipulated me in order to make sure Glenn would win? Guerrero was much more geared to "playing to win" than I was; for that matter so was Glenn. Moreover, Glenn, though younger than I, was more advanced as a pianist, and unquestionably he *deserved* to win. That was his beautiful, enthralling performance of the Prelude in b flat.

I recall a second "resentment." My first full solo recital during my studies with Guerrero took place on 3 December 1947, and on the same night Glenn was to make his first appearance on an orchestral subscription program, playing the Beethoven Concerto no. 1 in an out-of-town engagement with the Toronto Symphony Orchestra under MacMillan. Guerrero was always supportive of his pupils' performances, but this time he had to decide which of the two events he would attend, and he went to Hamilton to hear Glenn. It was the logical choice, as time has since assured me, however much my nervous younger self wishes he had been there to hear *me*. Glenn's advancement was, and of course *ought* to have been, of prime concern to his teacher.

In an interview, Claudio Arrau recollected meeting Gould, "when he was seventeen or eighteen. His teacher was a great friend of mine. He played for me at Guerrero's house. Guerrero didn't know what to do with this genius. I remember most distinctly what a terrific impression he made upon me. His facility and musical ability were remarkable even at that age. Guerrero asked me what course he should follow and I told him to let him alone."[26] Arrau is the only observer of the young Glenn Gould to suggest that Guerrero "didn't know what to do" in developing his talent. In his adult years, Gould made it known that he held a low opinion of Arrau's pianism.

After his first successes in the USA, as Gould became more and more of a celebrity, he found it less and less easy to accord Guerrero due credit for all he gave him. He started referring to him in interviews as "my

Guerrero and Gould, at the Gould family's cottage, ca. 1948 (Library and Archives Canada, Ottawa, Gould Collection), reproduced courtesy of the estate of Glenn Gould.

teacher," as if embarrassed to call him by name. After a while "My teacher" became characterized as a fussy old pedagogue, or as "a Latin," who obviously by "blood" was opposed to Gould's so-called Northern sensibilities. The remarks veer towards tastelessness, as in the "hunchback" example. In one invented story, which has been repeated many times in subsequent Gould annals, Gould claimed to have memorized the recorded performance by Artur Schnabel in order to prepare for the Beethoven Fourth Concerto performance. But this was an interpretation Guerrero did not favour. "My teacher," wickedly dominating, confiscates the discs (something it is impossible to imagine the real Guerrero ever doing, even if they were his property), but on the night of the concert the young upstart player does it Schnabel's way, in defiance. To anyone who attended the event, this is nonsense. Gould once told Stuart Hamilton he had learned nothing from Guerrero—to which Hamilton responded that, on the contrary, watching Gould play was like having a lesson with Guerrero.[27]

Gould's refusal to acknowledge Guerrero's guidance and influence carries over into the vast critical literature *about* Gould, so that Guerrero occupies a negligible or at best a distorted position in that literature. Edward W. Said's account of Gould's performing style includes the sweeping comment that Gould's only teacher (unnamed) "handed on practically none of his ideas to Gould."[28] In fact Gould learned most of his technical habits from Guerrero, though he eventually wilfully rejected many of Guerrero's aesthetic and interpretive ideas. Because Gould came to describe himself as self-taught, that is how other writers describe him in the approved literature, almost without exception. The historian Helmut Kallmann, who knew Gould in his CBC days and who organized the Gould exhibit at the National Library of Canada, Ottawa, in 1988, suggests that "self-taught" might be understood in the sense that we all need to absorb (teach ourselves, make part of ourselves) whatever skills our teachers teach us; but it is not certain that Gould and his chroniclers use the term that way. If a comparison is made between teacher and pupil, investigation suggests that the claim of self-education is far more valid of Guerrero than of Gould. One aim of study, Guerrero once told his pupil Alex Champoux, is to arrive at a point where you are "your own best teacher."[29]

It is difficult to assess Guerrero's reaction to the comments that Gould had begun making about their relationship. In April 1956 Gould gave his first Massey Hall solo concert after his tremendous US triumph of the previous year, and Guerrero did not attend. One report says he was in the audience but got up and walked out to protest Gould's exaggerated platform mannerisms. However this was not Guerrero's way: the story has to be untrue. What *is* true is that his pupil's platform mannerisms—his "antics," as Guerrero called them—became, by this time, distressing for the teacher to watch. He was nevertheless very proud of Gould's achievement. One much-quoted articulation of his feelings originated with Myrtle Rose Guerrero after Guerrero's death: "if Glenn feels he hasn't learned anything from me," Guerrero is supposed to have said, "it's the greatest compliment anyone could give me."[30] This much graciousness strikes me as uncharacteristic of Guerrero; the remark may represent an interpretation by his wife. A more likely summary is that of Kenneth Winters who said "Gould began to think he had done it all himself—and Guerrero let him think that."[31]

In the aftermath of Gould's untimely death in 1982, there were many LP releases of "forgotten" or "lost" performances by him. Some were genuine additions to the historical treasure. One spurious item was Turnabout TV-34793X, a 1983 release purporting to include privately recorded performances of four-hand piano music by Mozart, performed by Guerrero and the young Gould. The dubbings were taken from unlabelled discs made by Myrtle Rose Guerrero and Robert Finch following their recital of the complete Mozart duets in Toronto in 1947. Reading my description of this frankly fraudulent production, Sylvia Hunter, who had close contact with Myrtle Rose Guerrero in her last years, confirmed the players' identities: "Myrtle had told me…that she was sure the Mozart was played by Robert Finch and her, and not by Glenn and Mr. G."[32]

Ms. Hunter's memory of Guerrero's relationship with Gould in the later 1950s differs from the version usually accepted by Gould's biographers. If there was a "break," in the sense of a strong divergence of views, it did not mean they discontinued all contact. As she recalls, "I studied with Mr. G. full-time from '53–'57, and part time after that until his death, and Glenn sometimes phoned during my lessons and also attended some receptions at the Guerreros' home following student concerts."[33]

Ray Dudley's recollections of this period are similar. He remembers social gatherings where both Gould and Guerrero were present. For example, in the summer of 1958 or '59, when Fran and Ray Dudley went with the Guerreros to a Chinese restaurant in Orillia, they encountered Gould, who cordially invited them all to come back to his family cottage for an evening visit. The teenaged Arthur Ozolins was introduced to Gould at Guerrero's home in 1959. Pierrette LePage recalls from the late 1950s that Guerrero displayed a framed photo of the young Gould in his studio at Cottingham Street.[34]

The nine-year teacher-student relationship of Guerrero and Gould was tremendously productive. As he became not just a famous pianist but a worldwide household name (literally a registered trademark), Gould found he could not acknowledge his teacher—in fact, he denied him. For this, the psychological interpretations are part of Gould's story, not Guerrero's. For at least one writer (William Littler), Guerrero's *only* claim to distinction is that he was the teacher of Glenn Gould. It would be more accurate to reverse that statement: among Gould's many claims to distinction is that he started out as a pupil of Alberto Guerrero.

A Letter

When I was studying in Paris, I wrote often to Guerrero. He wrote less often, but the following letter, dated 18 January 1951, refers in a characteristic way to a number of personalities and musical issues.[35] This is the text in full:

Dear John,

Your letters have given us a great pleasure. Myrtle loves Paris and you seem to know exactly the kind of information I would enjoy. There is no word in them that has not found a responsive echo somewhere in me, and not the least your talk about meals and wines. As for your first contact with Mlle. and subsequent reactions to her extraordinary personality, I find fascinating and I thank you for having taken the trouble of telling me your experiences.[36]

Being such a bad correspondent, I hesitate to ask you to continue writing, realizing that one day you may give up as hopeless this one-way, lavish pouring of interest and friendship.

As I very seldom go out from the sunroom the interesting things that happen in Toronto pass without me knowing of them. I will have very little to tell you for that reason.

I remember you asking me about Copland's visit here. I did not go to hear his address in Convocation Hall but I went to Mazzoleni's cocktail party for him.[37] By the way, that is the only party I have been to this winter. The usual sort of affair. Many people trying to talk to him and very little time to do it. My turn came when the party was quite advanced. We talked about things and people we knew; of a friend of mine in South America, Domingo Santa Cruz, to whom he, as adjudicator in a competition, had given a prize and how the chilean press, or part of it, had connected that to the many drinks and dinners that this friend had been able to provide.

He mentioned your name and was going to say something when Ridout came to say goodbye.[38] With his usual air of importance and at the same time certain indifference, he said that he would have liked that Copland heard some of his compositions, but that being a composer he was a bad pianist and for the moment had no recordings available; so the occasion would have to be postponed. Copland listened with great interest, approved and disapproved in the right places and when Ridout left asked me what was the name of the man. Soon after Ridout came a good looking young woman. She asked Copland if the "baby" wanted to go home. He answered that he wanted to stay.

From there on more people came to talk to him and our little interview was over.

Later I have heard that some of our composers had shown him some of their products while he was here. To one of them who informed him that he had been studying with Milhaud and that Milhaud had liked the particular composition he was going to play, Copland is reported to have said "Yes, Milhaud would like that."[39]

I have been to two interesting concerts. In the Heliconian Club the violinist Schneider played the six unaccompanied suites by Bach. Superbly done. Perhaps with too much fervour and jewish pathos, though not of the bad kind. The other was a charming recital by Segovia.

Glenn's recital of modern music brought the rightup [sic] I include.[40] Glenn is so fascinated at the moment by the cleverness of the twelve tone composers in their arranging of tones and by the particular texture they obtain, that he is inclined to forget that the ultimate object of all this cleverness should be to produce form beyond the manipulation of the tone-row. The Krenek Sonata [no. 3], for instance impresses me as a neo-romantic composition in feeling with climaxes arranged very much in the way of the Prelude to Tristan, say. (I admit the analogy is somewhat far-fetched.) I mean

Alberto Guerrero, letter to John Beckwith, 18 January 1951: pages 7 and 9, of 10 (Collection J. Beckwith)

to say that in emotion the Sonata is not different from that and that it is this emotion what the listener must be getting.

I don't know how good his bassoon Sonata is. I imagine that I don't listen in the proper spirit, because one day, for instance, I made the remark that at one moment in which everything seemed to be pointing to a climax, the bassoon stopped—faded out, would be better—and failed to add anything to the moment. Glenn's answer was that all that could be done with [h]is tone-row had been done already and consequently there was nothing left for the bassoon to say.

At this moment comes to me a remark I read once that Mlle. Boulanger had made about a passage in the last movement of the Sonata by Strawinski in which the soprano has the theme in sixteenth notes and the bass has the same theme in eighth notes. Mlle. said that that was a "tour de force."

The only thing I find in the passage is that by ordinary standards of tonality the notes do not fit. There is no tonality to live up to. It is not, it seems to me, as when Bach does that, say, in the eighth fugue of the WTC [Well-Tempered Clavier]. In this case the double values add considerably to the emotional intensity of the last part of the fugue and seem to provide the only fitting frame for the expanding drive of the form.

I have no doubt that Mlle. is right but I would like very much to know in what consists the "tour de force" of Strawinski.

I see by your letters that you are one (or two, because I am sure Pamela is another,) of those people very much to my liking, who adore Paris good or bad, including the sentimental song in a small caffé [*sic*] at night and the hundreds of small little happenings of everyday.[41]

Sometime ago I received a letter from a friend I had not seen nor heard of for twenty five years. He says he remembers that in 1925 we sat for a chat near the statue of Verlaine in Paris. I remember that too. We had been in many places with this friend. In New York, in Amsterdam, in Havana, in Chile. But the first thing he remembers after twenty five years is to have been sitting by the statue of Verlaine in Paris.[42]

I have started my Bach lectures. Last Wednesday I played the 2 part inventions and next time I should continue with the 3 part and some of the WTC, etc.

I would think that there are about six people who come to these lectures because they are interested in the subject. Most of the others looked pretty bored. Some of the young girls seemed ready all the time to write something, a date, some definite fact. There was nothing they could write, apparently. Some would leave the room while I was playing.

Myrtle joins me in sending you and Pamela our best wishes.

A.G.

The Final Public Recital

On 16 November 1952, Guerrero performed a solo recital in the Hart House Sunday Evening series at the University of Toronto. He had been a solo or chamber-music performer in this series many times, starting in its second season, 1922–23. The two main numbers on this occasion were J.S. Bach's *Italian Concerto* and Schubert's Sonata in B flat, D. 960, with, separating them, a group of shorter pieces by Scarlatti and Brahms. In the following Tuesday's edition of the student newspaper *The Varsity,* an unfavourable review appeared whose author, Keith Rowe, was then a mathematics major at Victoria College.

The review began: "Of the six works, Mr Guerrero had memorized four—the four shortest—and this divided the concert into good and not-so-good classes, with the four short works in the former category." I remember a few seasons earlier hearing a wonderful performance of the Third Concerto by Beethoven in which the soloist, Myra Hess, played from the score. Rowe continued: "About the opening Bach *Italian Concerto*...the only good to be said is that the last movement was better than the first two." He added: "I recommend Landowska's recording." Even when describing some items with approval, the critic managed to incorporate negatives:

> The Capriccio in B minor and Intermezzo in B flat by Brahms, and two Sonatas (in G and E [most likely K. 427 and K. 380]) by Scarlatti, were excellently done. It is hard to decide which one of the four, if any, was the best, but the Capriccio was not far from it. Mr Guerrero's performance was crisp, cool, and brilliant....By repeating the Scarlatti G major Sonata as an encore, Mr Guerrero eliminated the technical errors which marred his first attempt; this performance was crisp, warm and brilliant; it bounced joyously up and down the keyboard and was fully delightful.

Turning to the Schubert Sonata, Rowe spoke of Guerrero's "loose performance," in which "technical details were slurred over, and melodies disappeared in a mass of seemingly uncontrolled sound. This was especially true of the first and third (Scherzo) movement[s]. But the Andante was given a quiet, flowing performance of a standard quite in contrast to the rest of the work."

The review was not so much opinionated as heavily judgmental—the goods and the not-so-goods; the annihilation of the Schubert performance; the quasi-authoritative (and totally nervy) recommendation of a recording. Having attended and greatly enjoyed the concert, I found this critique completely at odds with what I had heard. Guerrero, who was used to both praise and pannings in reviews throughout his professional life, told me he found this one offensive. The Hart House series was attractive—one played for a cultivated audience in a warm and friendly atmosphere, and this lent the invitation an agreeable artistic aspect (invitation rather than contract, because the honorarium was always small). It seemed to him both unfair and insulting that an undergraduate should publish such high-handed and ill-informed remarks afterwards. Although Guerrero made these observations rationally, with no angry explosion, I see now he was really hurt.

Rowe ended his piece by returning to his leitmotif: "It is to be hoped that [Guerrero] has the remaining two numbers memorized when he gives his public concert later this week." The "public concert" referred to was probably an Eaton Auditorium benefit concert for a private girls' school, St. Mildred's College, on 20 November. It appears to have been Guerrero's last performance before an audience.[43]

The Robert Finch Papers include the undated pencil manuscript of a short poem—inspired, a letter of enclosure says, by Guerrero's performance of the slow movement of the *Italian Concerto*. The poem depicts this elaborately ornamented piece as a translation from birdsong; the poet (signing only as "B.") adds: "and my mind said, it must have sounded exactly that [way] to Bach."[44]

six

The 1950s

At the start of the 1950–51 season, Guerrero's old chamber-music colleague, the cellist-composer Leo Smith, became music critic for the *Globe and Mail,* and at his invitation Guerrero contributed occasional concert reviews. Excerpts from his brief notices of recitals given in Massey Hall by José Iturbi and William Kapell will serve to illustrate Guerrero's style and approach—his emphasis on, and enthusiasm for the music, and, somewhat, his skepticism about its handlers.

Noting that Iturbi had not played in Toronto for ten years, Guerrero comments: "There is of course a great difference between the meticulous, almost perfectionist pianist of his early days and the tremendously popular, versatile pianist-conductor...and movie star who made his appearance in person" on this occasion. Iturbi's playing, he says,

> had that certain freedom and abandon which makes a performance sound like an improvisation. It is a great quality in a concert artist, if after a surprise or two the magnetism of his interpretation carries you with him through his flexible rubato, through the waves of crescendos and diminuendos without protest. This kind of playing is naturally more effective in romantic, impressionistic music, and more so in rhapsodies like the Hungarian by Liszt and Rhapsody in Blue by Gershwin....Perhaps it was a bit surprising to find it in the Mozart A Major Sonata. Being at the beginning of the program we were not yet ready to be carried along without protest.

Iturbi's performance of Ravel's *Jeux d'eau,* a work Guerrero had played innumerable times, "had all the tonal subtlety dear to the impressionists.

But the Greek god of the fountain did not laugh at the water tickling him, as Ravel suggests. This was a rather plaintive, sad god."[1]

Kapell's "altogether remarkable" recital was his first in Toronto, though he had previously been heard as soloist with the Toronto Symphony Orchestra. "Few listeners, unless they dislike modern idioms altogether, will ever forget his sensational performance of the Khatchaturian Concerto some three or four seasons ago." But Guerrero found the recital program more conservative: "those who had hoped that the visit of an outstanding interpreter of today's American musical thought was a marvellous opportunity to hear the new music genuinely played, were out of luck." Kapell's recording of Bach's Partita no. 4 in D (Phillips Classics 456–853–2) is notable for the exaggeratedly slow tempo of the Allemande movement. Of its performance on the Massey Hall program, Guerrero commented:

> The Allemande seemed of an extraordinary length. A richly ornamented cantilena unfolds itself over a harmonic structure that, though full of connecting and prolonged links, maintains an ample and far-reaching unity of purpose. The pianist seemed to have put all his attention in the ornamented cantilena upon which he lavished his most delicate pianissimos and varied tonal effects. At that moment, I agreed with Bach's contemporary, Rameau, who thought that the musical expression was really to be found in the harmony.

Debussy's *Children's Corner* was "exquisitely presented," and the Chopin Sonata (no. 3 in b, Opus 58) "brilliantly played, with great tonal contrasts": "After two or three minutes of pianissimo in the slow movement... the thunder of the finale seemed terrifying: all extremely well thought out and most efficiently done."[2]

Guerrero's intermittent association with the *Globe* ceased on Smith's death, after a brief illness, in April 1952, when the editors initiated a different arts-coverage policy.

The Guerreros' purchase, in the late 1940s, of a lakefront cottage at Victoria Point, near the town of Orillia, made them close neighbours of the Goulds. It became their summer home (with a small Chickering grand piano for practice) and a weekend retreat during the height of the teaching season. Glenn Gould described the place's value to them like this: "In December (the first weekend) the Guerreros still are going to Victoria Point. It has given him more enth[us]iasm than Ive ever seen in him before."[3] In the early 1950s they decided to change their residence in the city, and acquired a large old house at 177 Cottingham Street, in a residential enclave known locally as "the republic of Rathnelly." The move two kilometres north from the apartment on Grosvenor took place some time in late 1952 or early 1953.

Alberto Guerrero, a portrait by the photographer John Steele, 1950 (Library and Archives Canada, Ottawa, John Steele Collection)

Guerrero sat for his portrait by the well-known photographer John Steele in 1950. He sardonically remarked that he agreed to do so because the newspapers were "always asking for an up-to-date photo—in case you die." The print favoured by Steele showed Guerrero without his glasses, in a characteristic and quite animated facial expression. Guerrero rejected it, saying it made him look "like some French actor," and selected a more conventional pose. It happened that I had a sitting with Steele shortly after this, and heard first-hand how much the photographer had enjoyed his encounter with Guerrero. The rejected photo won a prize in a national exhibition the following year.

Guerrero's teaching in this decade attracted some outstandingly talented pupils, among them Paul Helmer, later a professor with the Faculty of Music at McGill University, Montreal; Edward Laufer, later a music theorist and professor at the University of Toronto; Patricia Perrin, later Patricia Krueger, the long-time keyboardist of the Toronto Symphony Orchestra; John McIntyre, professor of piano at the University of Missouri, Kansas City; Shirley Pethes, professor of piano pedagogy at West Chester University in Pennsylvania; Gordana Lazarevich, author, and professor of musicology at the University of Victoria; Arthur Ozolins, whose concert tours and recordings have made an international mark; Anahid Alexanian, Gould disciple and pianist-organizer in the early 1960s of Canada's first live

Pierrot lunaire; and R. Murray Schafer, the best-known Canadian composer of his generation. Schafer studied with Guerrero "for about a year in 1954," and recalls that his lessons focused less on piano performance and more on discussions of his developing literary interests. "[Guerrero] listened generously, and set me reading a lot of new authors…I adored this man for the breadth of his knowledge and understanding."[4] The description is reminiscent of the remarks made by another composer, Domingo Santa Cruz, about his studies with Guerrero forty years earlier.

A main topic of concern in Canada in the 1950s was the perceived need for public support of the arts. Guerrero took a progressive point of view. On listening to a radio broadcast devoted to chamber music by the emerging composer John Weinzweig in 1951, he said he thought it showed a new departure that merited cultivation and subsidy. For his part, in a kind of mock-bigotry, Weinzweig appreciated Guerrero's position in Toronto's musical circles, "because he wasn't English." Weinzweig's students for composition and analysis (e.g., R. Murray Schafer) went to Guerrero for piano lessons, while Guerrero's pupils (e.g., Gordana Lazarevich) went to him for theoretical study.

The last novel of the Canadian writer Robertson Davies, *The Cunning Man*, is set in Toronto in the early 1950s.[5] It is a *roman à clef* in which personalities in the world of the arts of that time appear under fictional names. An extended description of a musicale introduces participants who are recognizable as MacMillan, Kihl, Willan, Boris and Borina Hambourg, and Guerrero. The fictional names of the first four are more or less clever clues: Gow, the traditional Scottish fiddler; Gade, the Danish composer; Parry, the English composer and pedagogue; Moscheles, the German-Jewish composer and pianist. But the Guerrero character is named Augusto Da Chiesa, a puzzling invention. "Da Chiesa" is Italian for "of the church," from which one would hardly guess the agnostic Guerrero. Da Chiesa is careful about his diet, has a gifted young pupil "who will make them all sit up and take notice in a few years," and "has a mistress!" (although in the period suggested in the novel Guerrero and Rose were already married). Further, he "plays Scarlatti like an angel." This phrase appeared in a review of Guerrero's concert in Peterborough, Ontario, in the late 1940s; the reviewer was Robertson Davies. (Guerrero recounted that after the concert he had met Davies, then editor and columnist on the *Examiner.*) For mysterious reasons, perhaps having to do with legal protection, Davies later denied that the characters in *The Cunning Man* were based on actual people.[6]

The 1950s were a period of considerable expansion in Myrtle Rose's career. While continuing her expert work with children, individually and in classes, and her pedagogical courses at the University of Toronto, she was also developing some serious and talented advanced students, among whom Angela Hewitt, Tony Collacott, and the sisters Kathleen and Jane Solose all became prominent performers. A move to involve herself in volunteer promotional activity (in the early 1950s with a committee of the Toronto Mendelssohn Choir) was short-lived; Guerrero thought she could use her time more effectively.[7]

In 1957, his pupil Janet Horton married Michael Kilburn, a member of a well-respected Toronto musical dynasty. At the wedding reception, Guerrero proposed the toast to the bride—despite his usual aversion to public speaking.

In May 1957 the Guerreros travelled to New York to attend a major performance by one of his favourite former pupils, Ray Dudley. Dudley was soloist with the New York Philharmonic under Franco Autori in Carnegie Hall on 3 and 4 May. The work was Rachmaninov's Concerto no. 3. Before embarking on his first trip to New York in nearly twenty years, Guerrero had made, in April, a one-day, round-trip excursion to Ottawa in order to update his travel documents. The Guerreros joined several other Dudley fans forming a Canadian party in the Philharmonic audience. Dudley's success, as a finalist in the International Geneva Competition in 1952, as a touring performer under Columbia Artists management, and eventually as a professor at the School of Music at Indiana University in Bloomington, was highly gratifying to Guerrero. They remained good friends, and Dudley became one of the main inheritors of Guerrero's teaching style, both in his own studio work and in many teacher workshops.

As another former student enjoying his friendship, I have memories of many contacts with Guerrero in the 1950s. While I was performing less, devoting more time to composing and teaching, I had nevertheless a few coaching lessons. He and Myrtle Rose Guerrero came to dinner one evening in 1953 to our third-floor flat in the Dovercourt-College area of Toronto; he was, I remember, amazed that I was practising on a tiny upright piano that had had to be dismantled in order to go up the stairs. There were further wonderful get-togethers at Cottingham and at my later home a few blocks away. Although Guerrero was fond of food and wine, like the fictional Da Chiesa he was not only moderate in his habits but watchful of his diet in those years; on one occasion, he went out to the kitchen to inspect some dish or other and asked us to exclude the mushrooms.

As a scriptwriter for music programs on CBC Radio, I inaugurated in 1953 a series of half-hour broadcasts of recorded new music, choosing the most "avant-garde" LPs and tapes I could locate—a daring venture at that period. After the first program in the series, featuring music by Varèse and Schoenberg, Guerrero sent me a short note of commendation.

I gave a few performances of the Sonata (1924) by Igor Stravinsky, and analyzed this work with my students. In discussions of it with Guerrero, he thought the *grupetti* of the slow movement were "reminiscent of Gottschalk." The revival of interest in the music of this American pianist-composer (1829–69) was just beginning, but I wondered if, from the impact of Gottschalk's South American exile years (including a sojourn in Chile), some memories had remained in Guerrero's youth. (In researching this book, however, I located no Gottschalk performances by Guerrero.) Another slow movement, that of Prokofiev's Seventh Sonata, had for him the melodic flavour of a sentimental pop song; he mentioned for comparison Jerome Kern's "Smoke Gets in Your Eyes."

The topic of innovation in piano writing came up: in the vastness of the instrument's repertoire it seemed as if everything had been done. Guerrero cited two early-twentieth-century passages—the double glissandos of Ravel's *Alborada del grazioso* and a scale passage in double notes in the finale of Prokofiev's Third Concerto (the fingers covering two notes each)—as among the last really new devices. When an anthology of Henry Cowell's inside-the-piano pieces was published, along with an LP of the composer playing them, Guerrero was keenly interested, and approved my idea of encouraging some of the young pianists to include them in their recitals.

In student days, I had always appreciated his criticisms of my compositions. In the fall of 1958 Pamela Terry and I went to his home and sang and played through for him the score of a one-act opera I had completed that summer. His comments were, as always, generous and precise. The opera, *Night Blooming Cereus,* was introduced the following April on CBC Radio, and no doubt Guerrero heard it. I recall he found the finale a contemporary take on the eighteenth-century form of the chorale-prelude. In retrospect it seems odd that he never mentioned his own early experiences composing for the lyric theatre. I was also working on a newer project that was a work for piano and orchestra, and I read through the completed first movement at his piano in early 1959. I thought the ideas might be considered too reflective of the influence of Copland, whose Piano Sonata I had played under coaching by Guerrero in 1950. Guerrero said yes, the influence was probably obvious, but not a bad feature. He thought I had treated the medium rather in the manner of Schumann in his Piano Concerto, a work we both loved. I was not conscious of this, but could see his point, and, remembering that Schumann had originally called his work a Fantasy, I chose the title "Concerto Fantasy" for mine, dedicating it to Guerrero. It was not completed until after he died.

Guerrero was no longer performing in public in the later 1950s when William Aide studied with him. Aide recalls that he seldom played at his lessons. My own lessons, a decade earlier, were constantly enlivened by his on-impulse readings—pieces he was practising or that he thought I ought to learn. Ray Dudley similarly recollects that, when he was a student, "Guerrero often played for me works he was suggesting as repertoire. The last time I had a lesson was the year he passed away [1959]. He sat down and played Franck's Prelude, Chorale, and Fugue from beginning to end. It was stunning."[8]

A Funeral

Guerrero was full of enthusiasm for the new teaching season in September 1959. Young students enrolling for the first time included several outstanding talents he said he eagerly looked forward to working with—especially the remarkable thirteen-year-old Arthur Ozolins.

Towards the end of October he had to undergo an operation for a hernia of the esophagus. Though he was no hypochondriac, care for his own physical well-being was a fundamental habit with him, and this was his first hospital stay. There had been a bout of illness in the summer of 1942,[9] and prior to that there is correspondence hinting at a period of mild intestinal troubles in 1930–31. His additional weight in the late 1950s may have put his health at a certain risk. The hernia procedure, not of major concern even in a person of Guerrero's age (seventy-three), went satisfactorily; but he developed serious complications that were described as peritonitis, became suddenly weaker, and died within a few days. During his decline, and as the hospitalization lengthened, Myrtle Rose gathered a group of students in the living room at Cottingham—William Aide, Pierrette LePage, and Arthur Ozolins among them—and had them play for each other.[10] The news of his death, on 7 November, came as a shock.

There were obituary tributes in the local newspapers and in music periodicals in Canada and in Chile, as well as brief notices in American journals (*Musical America, Variety*).

The funeral ceremony was an occasion of deep sadness—and also of absurdity. It took place in the small chapel of an upscale mortuary on St. Clair Avenue near Yonge Street (the building no longer exists). Just a week or two previously, I had attended the funeral of another prominent musician, the violinist Géza de Kresz, in a Hungarian church on Bathurst Street, and was appalled that no one had given any thought to the music of the service, which as a result was ill-chosen, droopy, and incompetently played. Myrtle Rose was grateful when I offered to make enquiries about possible music for Guerrero's funeral, and the young organist Douglas Bodle said he felt honoured to play: his selection of Bach organ chorales lent an appropriate musical ambience, despite the dire limitations of the chapel instrument.

Aksel Schiøtz, the Danish singer who had recently come to Toronto to teach, was leaving the Royal Conservatory as I was; he was on his way to the funeral also, so we sat together. Schiøtz had met Guerrero only a few times, but recognized him as an important personality ("a great man" was how he put it).

The chapel was packed. The casket, front and centre, was fortunately closed. Bert and Flo Gould had helped Myrtle Rose with the arrangements and, given the Guerreros' lack of church affiliation, had invited their United Church pastor to conduct the service. (Glenn was on tour and did not interrupt his schedule to attend.) The minister had an earnest and kindly manner, but he was at a disadvantage having never known Guerrero, and his religious tone struck those who *had* known him as quite unfortunate. The prepared eulogy was not only overly long but it used language that bore hardly any relation to the man we were remembering—a man the minister familiarly referred to as "our brother." In the front pew on the right, a composed and plainly dressed Myrtle Rose Guerrero was accompanied by her long-time friends Norman and Betty Endicott, with the Goulds just behind. Opposite, in the front pew on the left, in evident distress, sat Mélisande Irvine, and, next to her, in black with a heavy veil, an older woman known to hardly anyone in the crowd—Lily Wilson Guerrero. At the conclusion of the eulogy, this figure dramatically moved forward and draped herself over the casket for a moment, then raised herself and slowly led the way out of the chapel. The unexpected gesture—a prayer? an embrace?—added discomfort and puzzlement to the feelings of sadness on the part of the rest of the assembly. At the exit, several of the students were crying. William Aide's poem describing this bizarre farewell gathering includes the lines: "the ludicrous funeral instrument, / the bad 'our brother' oration."[11]

Shortly before Guerrero died, Glenn Gould gave a radio interview in California. Most of his broadcast interviews were scripted in advance by him, but this one was not. The published transcript includes some of Gould's most negative remarks about Guerrero.[12] Referring to him again as "my teacher," he describes his style of playing as overpedalled and "extraordinarily whimsical" in phrasing—wildly inaccurate criticisms. The succeeding paragraphs of the interview drift off into incoherence. One is left with the impression that Gould was under a heavy mental strain.

R. Murray Schafer, then studying in Europe, reacted to the news of Guerrero's death by composing a short work for string orchestra, *In Memoriam Alberto Guerrero*.[13] It is not so much a musical portrait of the man as an intensely dramatic abstract interlude. Schafer's program note calls it "a tribute to a great musician, whose influence I shall never forget."

"Boswell"

The English-born conductor Boyd Neel came to Toronto in 1953 to take up a senior appointment as dean of the newly reorganized Royal Conservatory of Music. He came to know Guerrero and was a guest at Guerrero's home on several occasions. On Guerrero's death, he published an obituary notice in the Conservatory's *Monthly Bulletin,* which appears here as Appendix 2. It was later reprinted in an abridged Spanish translation in Chile.[14]

Written in the hyperbolic style Neel used effectively as a public spokesperson for the conservatory, the article reiterates in exaggerated form many inaccurate details concerning Guerrero's early life—that his family had a long-established prominence in Santiago's cultural circles, that he founded and conducted Santiago's first orchestra, and so on. Neel, who is unlikely ever to have heard Guerrero play, wrongly depicts Guerrero as having had "no ambitions to become a virtuoso pianist," and—in a further distortion based on the limited travelling of Guerrero's later years—he states that Guerrero "hated travel." Neel also typically reproduces the redundancy that Guerrero "*constantly* received *many* requests" to return to Chile.

Three paragraphs are devoted to an intimate description of Guerrero's ideas on teaching. A favourite subject in conversations with Guerrero, Neel reveals, was "the discrepancy between performance and technique." He nowhere says that this is the precise title of Guerrero's 1950 article in the same periodical (see Appendix 1). His detailed quotations are all taken holus-bolus from that article, as even a cursory comparison of the two texts makes clear. The quotations are disguised as minutely recalled and savoured memories of a Boswell-like devotee: "he would say," "he would quote," "he never tired of quoting," "another axiom to which I often heard [him] refer," "one of his favourite expressions."

Guerrero did not bore hearers with "favourite expressions" and, contrary to Neel's characterization of him, he had no tiresome habit of talking in "axioms." In Guerrero's article, he acknowledges, as the source for its quotations from Mersenne and from Anaxagoras, a 1949 article by the French musicologist Marc Pincherle, but Neel chooses to ignore this acknowledgement.

The Neel obituary, in sum, amounts to a breathtaking plagiarism. The author generously calls Guerrero "irreplaceable," a "great gentleman," and "among the great teachers of our time," but his own autobiography contains not one reference to Guerrero.[15]

Legacy

"Guerrero cultivated a whole generation of musicians. Though he appeared to me only as a master-teacher of piano, he profoundly affected the musical awareness of…composers.…Established performers and pedagogues…came to him for counsel. Musicians in other niches studied with [him].… Guerrero is revered…as the unsung progenitor of our nation's musical culture."[16] This appraisal by William Aide echoes the kind of position Guerrero is described as having in Chile forty-five years before. At Guerrero's death, Alfonso Leng recalled his powerful presence as a performer, and especially the advice and encouragement he gave to his composer-colleagues; summing up, he called Guerrero "the man who outlined the path of Chilean music from 1912 on," adding that, "without his intelligent influence and extraordinary musical sensitivity, the progress of music in Chile would have been different."[17]

"But," Aide adds significantly, "it was all done privately. There were no public conducting or administrative posts…There are no recordings of what must have been [his] astonishing recitals."[18]

Guerrero's influence, felt in so many spheres, was based on one-on-one contacts, with pupils, with consulting individuals, with colleagues. Margaret Sheppard Privitello described him as conscious of his own superior abilities, modest and self-effacing in manner, intolerant of pomposity in others, and liking to maintain control of personal exchanges, without appearing to dominate. To a later pupil, Bruce Mather, he was "a quiet man of few words [–] but carefully chosen words, precisely to the point, often in the form of a question, usually a question I could not answer but that forced me to fruitful reflection."[19]

During the conservatory crisis of 1952, MacMillan called Guerrero in distress late one evening, and begged him to come to his house for a chat. He needed advice, and Guerrero was the person he turned to. Other players in the political battle were changing their positions, seemingly in response to personal advantage. Guerrero's counsel, which MacMillan followed, was that if he wanted to maintain his considerable prestige he should stay true to his convictions. Guerrero's role in the discussions was, characteristically, a private one.[20]

At the start of my own teaching experience, he talked with me about the intangibles of the teaching process—the tricky, unpredictable transfer, not so much of factual information as of know-how, of attitude, from one consciousness to another. For R. Murray Schafer, Guerrero was "one of the few musicians from whom a student could get ideas beyond music."[21] Malcolm Troup, like Schafer, records that often the lesson time would be occupied with conversation about literature, painting, or philosophy, aimed

Alberto Guerrero at the piano in his Cottingham Street home, Toronto, ca. 1957, photographer unknown (Collection Pierrette LePage)

at formation of the pupil's intellectual habits. But the teaching act could also be directed on precise points of piano playing. Aide, again, has recorded one example of a breakthrough in his studies, when Guerrero suddenly, by holding his arm to free his fingers, helped him produce the rapid flow of Chopin's Étude in a, Opus 25, no. 11 ("Winter Wind"): as he puts it in his poem, "You held my arm / is all I remember."[22] Laurence Morton said, of his lessons in the late 1940s, "[Guerrero] turned me completely around, pianistically speaking, and…I could never have had a career in piano without his immense influence and direction."[23]

A lesson with Guerrero followed no formula, though it would always have a form; was this perhaps what he meant by having "no method"? Lessons were varied, as Sylvia Hunter remembers: "Sometimes he would lean back in his chair and say 'play me something,' and would not say a word until the piece was finished. Other times we would not get past more than the first three or four bars of a work. Still other times we would talk for the entire hour, not necessarily about music.…Occasionally we would work on various exercises for the entire lesson."[24] From the same late (Cottingham Street) period, Pierrette LePage recounts the circumstances of her lessons with Guerrero like this: "I came directly from school for my lesson, and would arrive an hour early—the door was never locked. I was allowed to practise before he came downstairs…[The] lesson was sometimes spent talking about different things—We would have tea…. When my lesson was the last one of his day, I would walk his dog 'Pancha' with him, around the block."[25] Edward Laufer's reminiscences are even more detailed, beginning with his first meeting with Guerrero:

I was a little nervous, but he put me at ease....He asked me what I had been working on; I mentioned a few pieces, and added that I had also been practising various finger exercises. "Play me one of the exercises." I was surprised that he wanted to hear an exercise rather than real music. I started something in double thirds. After a few seconds, not more, he stopped me. "Do you hear you are not playing the thirds quite together?" I had never noticed...I started again. "Which note, the upper or the lower, do you wish to be louder—or both the same?" This at once brought home to me that the blind, mechanical repetition of exercises, or musical passages, had no meaning or use or benefit: one had to start with a mental image of what one wanted, and then listen intently....

At this lesson, or a subsequent one, he gave me a quick movement to play, I think from the G major Partita, and despite earnest practising my right hand did not do too well. G. came over and pressed down on my right wrist: in my effort to combat the pressure, the fingers—much to my amazement—acquired a previously unknown lightness, accuracy, and clarity. G. explained that this was playing from the fingers only, without arm weight...[He] had various methods to get this idea across, and quite unconventional methods, I should think. One had to do with weights: in my case, heavy metal rings, such as those used in plumbing, suitably padded, placed around the wrists, to train the forearms what it felt like to play without arm weight; also—a specially shaped table, upon which the arms rested, so that the fingers and wrists were once again on their own....

I always had the feeling that each time I had a lesson, G. had learned something further, and the sense of studying with a teacher who himself was constantly learning something new was exhilarating...There was a certain spot [in the Fourth Ballade of Chopin] which required a trill to be played with the fourth and fifth (or possibly the third and fourth) fingers, which worried me, understandably, and I fluffed it. G. told me to get up and open the door. "You see," he said after I had turned the handle, "you did not think about it: you just turned the doorknob." It was the same with the trill. I repeated the passage, without the crippling worry, and it actually turned out tolerably well....

I recall an occasion when, arriving at his house a bit too early and waiting discreetly in the hallway, I could overhear some of the lesson of the student before me: the opening G-major chord of the Beethoven Fourth Concerto. I heard an untidy sound: the student at the better of the two grands—and it sounded like a student's playing, but I couldn't quite explain why. Then, on the other, weaker piano, G. played the chord. This one chord—and it was wonderful, magical! Then the student: poor, unclear, not right. Then G. again. Then the student. This went on for quite some time. Each time G.'s chord was just right, and the student's was clearly a student's attempt—but it got better....For me, the session was memorable and highly instructive: it had to do with achieving control, with realizing the sonority one had in one's imagination, with knowing exactly how to do this, each time, as G. did. Nothing had to be said.[26]

Guerrero once said to William Aide "I should have got you when you were ten"—a reminder of his ideas on the early formation of technique and also of his repeated successes with teenaged talents such as Maunder, Clemens, Samaloff, Gould, and Perrin. Pierrette LePage was, he told another pupil, the only one who came to him "with no bad habits." His patient and varied approach with younger pupils is evident in the quotation from LePage ("We would have tea"). When Ray Dudley, at seventeen living in a rooming-house in Toronto's east end, caught the flu, Guerrero and his wife nursed him in their home for two weeks. Dudley recalls his teacher's further kindness: "At the end of my 1st year I failed [a] technical exam—I passed the etudes...but stumbled through my scales—I was nervous....After what I thought was a horrible exam, [Guerrero] took me for a long walk..., talking to me in a positive way, analysing what happened etc and talking about having to do the exam over and how best to prepare for it. By the time I got back to [his] apartment I felt 100% better."[27]

Guerrero the teacher was resourceful and inspiring—and obviously devoted to his pupils' human development. As Mary Wilson Dell recalls, "The most exciting experiences in my lessons...were when [Guerrero] sat at the other piano and we had a dialogue of souls." Dell calls Guerrero "this open-hearted, passionate, caring man," and adds, "He would have made a good therapist!"[28]

"No recordings"—? Well, almost none. There are exactly two surviving recorded examples of Alberto Guerrero's performances that can be verified. The shoddy LP from Turnabout containing the mis-attributed Mozart duets also reproduces his performance of J.S. Bach's *Italian Concerto,* evidently from his CBC broadcast of this work in the fall of 1952;[29] and around 1940, as a birthday present for his daughter, he cut two sides of a 78-rpm disc containing the following pieces: Scarlatti: Sonata in E, K. 380; Liszt: *Valse oubliée*; and Granados: *La maja y el ruiseñor.* This second recording, dubbed onto a compact disc, now forms part of the Guerrero collection.

The Bach performance is enjoyable, though poorly recorded. One can appreciate his sustained quasi-vocal delivery of the slow movement, and especially the value he places on the harmonies of the accompanying left-hand lines, and his finale, though not as irrepressibly fast as the later recording by Glenn Gould, suggests by various details that it may have been

Gould's model.[30] The birthday disc, though meticulously played, shows signs of rushing, under the rigid confines of the three-to-four-minutes' 78-rpm format: for example, the repeats in the Scarlatti are omitted, something Guerrero would never have done in a public rendition of this piece. All three selections are typical of his repertoire—one of his favourite Scarlatti sonatas, an off-beat late Liszt work, and a beloved Granados example, the last especially sumptuous in delivery.

These are the only hints identified so far by which the power of his pianism can be judged by present and future generations. Persistent enquiries in the CBC Toronto archives and in the National Archives, Ottawa (where certain recordings of earlier CBC broadcasts are housed), have yielded nothing further, and no recordings were reported from Myrtle Rose Guerrero's estate.

Lily Wilson Guerrero died in Toronto in 1972, aged eighty-three, of cancer. Antony Irvine and his family, Guerrero's grandson and great-grandchild, now live in Puerto Vallarta, Mexico.

Myrtle Rose Guerrero remarried, in the middle 1960s, with Richard Knox-Leet, a retired naval commander. He managed her summer piano-pedagogy courses, which continued to operate for almost twenty years at Geneva Park, Orillia, near the vacation home they retained. They moved from Cottingham Street to a split-level house in Oakville, thirty kilometres west of Toronto on the Lake Ontario shore. She continued teaching—pedagogy classes at the University of Toronto and later also at McMaster University, Hamilton, as well as private lessons and children's classes in Oakville—and kept up an active routine even after Dick Knox-Leet's death (5 August 1987), by which time she was well into her eighties. She died in a nursing home in Oakville, diagnosed with Alzheimer's disease, on 11 August 1995, aged eighty-nine.

Various events have continued periodically to draw attention to Guerrero's legacy.

In 1978 I served on the adjudication panel for the Alberto Guerrero Memorial Prize, a $2,000 award for a new piano composition; my fellow judges were Oskar Morawetz and Robert Finch. The competition, initiated by Herbert and Mélisande Irvine, was administered by the Canadian Music Centre, and the prize went to the Vancouver composer Edward Artiega for his *Venturi* for two pianos. Entries in the competition were disappointingly few, and plans to offer the award annually had to be abandoned.

A more resounding venture was the one-day reunion of Guerrero's former pupils, on 25 October 1990, at the University of Toronto music faculty. The event was entitled "Remembering Alberto Guerrero." Over one hundred attended, of whom slightly more than half signed the attendees' list (see Appendix 3).[31] Many had travelled from other parts of Canada and the USA for the occasion; both Myrtle Rose Guerrero and Mélisande Irvine were honoured guests. There was a display of programs and photographs, a panel discussion, and, in the evening, a concert by six pianists: Paul Helmer, Arthur Ozolins, William Aide, Ray Dudley, and the two-piano team of Pierrette LePage and Bruce Mather. The program consisted of:

1. Sonata in C, Opus 2, no. 3, Beethoven (Helmer)
2. Sonata for two pianos (1970), Mather (LePage and Mather)
3. Two Mazurkas, Opus 17, no. 1 (B flat) and no. 4 (a), and Scherzo in b, Opus 20, Chopin (Ozolins)
4. *Les sons et les parfums tournent dans l'air du soir,* Debussy, and *Ondine,* Ravel (Aide)
5. Sonata in E flat, Hob. xvi/52, Haydn, and *Funérailles,* Liszt (Dudley) (Excerpts from the program essay appear as Appendix 4.)

Kenneth Winters's CBC Radio documentary series on outstanding music teachers devoted a program to Guerrero and his legacy, broadcast on 5 November 1996. It included excerpts from new interviews with Aide, Ozolins, Stuart Hamilton, and me, as well as from archival interviews with Gould. There being no available recordings of Guerrero's own playing, the musical illustrations were taken from recorded repertoire by Gould, Aide, and Gerald Moore, and as a finale R. Murray Schafer's *In Memoriam Alberto Guerrero* was played in full.

For TV Ontario's television series *A Scattering of Seeds* in 2001, Patricia Fogliato produced a half-hour documentary about Guerrero, entitled "The Music Teacher." The series took as its theme the rich contributions to Canadian life of individuals from other countries. Fogliato conducted new interviews with Hamilton, me, Aide, Dudley, and Mélisande Irvine. For music, there were piano excerpts by several of the interviewees, as well as samplings from Guerrero's "birthday" recording (Liszt, Scarlatti). Visuals included material from the Glenn Gould archives in the National Library, Ottawa, and from Mélisande Irvine's collection, and the sound track also introduced short passages from Guerrero's writings. Originally shown in May 2001, the program has been repeated several times.

One statement in Boyd Neel's obituary appears to be no exaggeration: "[the students], one and all, adored him." The effect of his personality, the pains he took as a teacher, his habitual kindness, for many also his deeply musical performances—have left lasting impressions to which former pupils (contacted during the preparation of this biography) bear tribute in a variety of ways, all with affection:

Ray Dudley: "The wisest man I ever knew."

John McIntyre: "The most inspiring, encouraging, and insightful teaching I ever had from any teacher."

Colleen Sadler: "He had such a way of making you feel that you were very capable, and were able to accomplish more and more."

Ray Dudley: "Miraculously he would make me play better with each lesson."

Paul Helmer: "He was an inspiration for his unorthodox approach—'All is fair in love and war and piano playing!' sticks in my mind."

Bruce Mather: "I found my lessons very enriching. He never said much, but whatever he said surprised me…and made me think a great deal about what I was doing. What better description of a fine pedagogue?"

John McIntyre: "He seemed like the most focused, supportive, and friendly audience I ever had."

Pierrette LePage: "A great teacher; he let all his students be themselves— they all played differently."

To his daughter, Guerrero was "an original."[32] There is plentiful evidence of his originality and extraordinary success as a teacher of piano playing—in testimonies from pupils, and in recordings such as Gould's complete Schoenberg and almost-complete Bach, Aide's complete Chopin Études and Preludes, and Dudley's complete Haydn sonatas, in all of which Guerrero's example and inspiration are manifest. Of his originality and formidable achievement as a performer, the evidence lies (regrettably) *only* in testimonies, but they are unquestionably persuasive. In time, such sentiments may develop a historical counteraction against the many erroneous versions of the Guerrero story that have been allowed to circulate.

From the distortions in Shakespeare's *Richard III,* it was necessary to form a Richard Plantagenet Society, devoted to researching the true story of that maligned monarch. Do we perhaps need a similar restorative vigilante group on behalf of Alberto Guerrero?

His own response to that notion would no doubt be a great roar of laughter.

appendix 1

Alberto Guerrero, "The Discrepancy between Performance and Technique"

I was playing in a recital many years ago and afterwards a student of mine said to me: "You don't play in the same way that you teach. For instance, you teach that the fingers should be kept in such a position, that the wrist should be at a certain level, that the elbows and the shoulders should be this way or the other; and then, when you play you don't obey any of your rules."

Though not quite convinced of the truthfulness of my reply, I said something about the fact that when one plays one is intent on presenting the music to the listener, trying to discover the emotion one feels and, if possible, transmit it to the audience so that the performance will have fulfilled its purpose, and that that was enough to occupy one's attention, leaving no room for thinking with what finger or in what position a note should be played.

That seems true enough. If we come to make the audience feel the emotion at the very moment in which we are discovering it in ourselves, fresh and animated by a new-born vitality, we should have given that something which is more than the notes, the time-values, the structure of the piece; we should have said something.

The problem aroused by my student's question remained still unsolved, though; and for a long time I thought of it until it formulated itself in this way: "Is it possible that when I teach the technique of the fingers and the wrist and the arms, and I make the student practise the five-finger exercise, and the passing of the thumb, and the firmness of the nail joint, the weight touch, and the musical touch, and the hundreds of things that we consider our duty to submit the student to; is it possible, I repeat (very much afraid of the turn that my sentence is taking), that all this analysis be in the way of the final purpose of making music at the piano?"

The discrepancy between performance and technique has been observed many times. It would be interesting to recall a few cases. One of the best-known instances appears to centre around Franz Liszt: his pupils have stated that he taught to play octaves from the wrist lifting the hand exaggeratedly and throwing it to the keys; but, they say, when he played his famous octave passages he "shook the octaves out of his sleeve."

One of the most successful pianists of today, who studied with Martin Krause (a pupil of Liszt of great reputation in the first part of the century) was showing me some time ago how, according to Krause, Liszt taught to produce the tone with a vigorous, thrusting movement of the forearm. This contrasts with the description of Théophile Gautier, the French writer. In one of Liszt's concerts in Paris, according to Gautier, "his hands came and went 'kneading' the ebony and ivory of the keyboard."

In all artistic endeavours—and performance is an artistic endeavour—analysis is decomposing, disintegrating. When we analyze a piece of music and we divide it and subdivide it in sections, sentences, phrases, motives, we destroy its wholeness, its coherence. The performer reintegrates these elements, reconstructs the piece in a new synthesis that will have the seal of his personality. And, if he is a real artist, he will recreate the composition and discover his emotion with the audience.

The same thing happens with our technique. We analyze our tools. We describe our fingers, hands, and arms as levers and apply to them the mechanical laws of leverage. We study their anatomy; what they are made of—the bones, the joints, the muscles; their physiology; how they work; relaxation, contraction. Some go so far as to give some muscles the exclusive function of producing a certain movement (a theory repudiated by scientific study).

But, as Dr. Alexis Carrel has said in his book *L'homme, cet inconnu*, the mechanical hand, the anatomical hand, the physiological hand, are not the hand; the integrated hand is much more than that: our hand is part of our mind.

Through our sensitive nervous system our hands will tell us, if we only put attention to their messages, how much pressure the piano key will need for the amount of tone we want, or in what position we can reasonably expect to be able to depress certain keys at a given time.

In ordinary life our hands are miraculously accurate. With my students I make an experiment that never fails. On a table, within easy reach of their hands, I put small objects of different shape and weight. All the student has to do is to lift each object a few inches from the table and put it back in the same place where it was before. It invariably happens that the judging of the object is very accurate. And not only that: the position of the hand and fingers is most efficient and corresponds exactly with what I would like to see when they are at the piano—that is, that, each object having a different shape, the position is different for each one. Most interesting also is the fact that the arm and, if the student is standing up, the body, initiate the movement for each object to be taken.

This would really mean that when the fingers are used in a group, as in a chord, the arm and even the body should initiate the movement. And what are our chords and broken chords and finger passages but groups of keys to be taken with one initial movement every time the thumb intervenes?

Now we may go back to the beginning of this article and suggest that the discrepancy between the teaching of technique and the actual performance comes from too much emphasis on the decomposition of the act of playing—action of the fingers, hand, and arms taught independently; and not enough thought given to the integration of the movement, that is, our hands as part of the mind collaborating in the discovery of the artistic emotion and its expression.

In other words, the technique to be useful to the performer must have the same integral grasp of the means to be employed as the performer must have of the composition to be played.

To conclude, let me say that it is not new to attribute to the hand the qualities of the mind. Father Mersenne, the author of *L'Harmonie universelle*, stated in the eighteenth century [*sic*] that the art, science, and industry of the hand are so great that the hand may be called one of the principal instruments of wisdom and of reason. And he quotes from Bassel (author of a treatise on the lute), who traces to the ancient Greek Anaxagoras the opinion that "human wisdom resides in the hand, although human beings should be considered wise not merely because they have hands, but rather they have been given hands because they are supposed to be wise, in order to be able to execute the dictates of art and reason." (See article by M. Pincherle in the *Musical Quarterly,* April 1949.)

NOTE: This article originally appeared in the Royal Conservatory of Music's *Monthly Bulletin* (October 1950): 2–3.

appendix 2

Boyd Neel, "Alberto Guerrero"

The sudden death of Alberto Guerrero was not only a grievous blow to the Royal Conservatory, but a disaster for Canada and Canadian music. His influence had not only been felt in this country, but also on the international scene, and his loss is irreparable.

Born in Chile, he began his professional life in Santiago, where the Guerrero family had for years been famous in musical circles. In a recent article in the journal published by the University of Chile, his name is mentioned as one of the chief figures of the Chilean school at the beginning of the century. At this time the musical life of Chile was beginning to acquire an individual style and the opera and the symphony orchestra were coming into their own. Guerrero grew up with this transplanted European atmosphere as his background and he acquired a culture which was to prove invaluable in later years.

In Chile he commenced his musical activities as a pianist, composer, and music critic and I do not think it is generally known that he composed many songs and an opera, all of which were very successful. When still quite a young man, he was involved in the musical life of his country to such an extent that a writer of the period described him as being indispensable to the Chilean musical scene and goes on to say that Guerrero was the chief figure in giving birth to the Chilean national music movement. It was he who organized and conducted the first orchestra in Santiago and, at about this time, he published a fine book on modern harmony. His contemporaries were Domingo Santa Cruz and Alphonso [sic] Leng, both of whom also became famous as pioneers in Chilean musical life.

He had no ambitions to become a virtuoso pianist, but so enjoyed giving concerts and taking part in ensemble work that these activities brought him to New York at quite an early stage in his career. From New York it was only a step to Toronto, where he was invited to teach at the Hambourg Conservatory. It was not long, however, before Dr. Vogt had persuaded him to join the staff at the conservatory, where he remained until his death. He never returned to his native country although, throughout his life, he constantly received many requests to do so.

His fame as a teacher of international standing came late in his career. For years he had done excellent work, but was little known outside Canada. It was the astounding success of Glenn Gould which finally put him among the great teachers of our time. Gould was the first of a series of brilliant pupils trained by Guerrero in his later years. He thus leaves behind him a great tradition of piano playing in this country.

"An extremely cultured and courteous gentleman" would seem to be a good description of this lovable man. A lone wolf among the teachers of Toronto, he rarely appeared in public, or even at the conservatory, since all his teaching was done in his beautiful home. He visited New York only once in the last twenty years and that was to hear his pupil Ray Dudley play a concerto with the Philharmonic. He hated travel and was never happier than when at his cottage near Orillia, entertaining a few intimate friends. He was a splendid raconteur and could discuss any aspect of the arts with profound knowledge. His reading was extensive and he was a real connoisseur of pictures, good food, and wine. An evening at Guerrero's home took one back into the atmosphere of the Proustian salons of the turn of the century. I think the word "civilized" most adequately describes this great gentleman.

As to his teaching method, it is almost impossible to define. He always maintained that he had no such thing—that each pupil was taught in a different way according to his nature. When one could get him to discuss this point, the discrepancy between performance and technique was the subject which usually came to the fore. This was the thing that intrigued him most. He would quote the student who came up to him in his early days after a recital and said: "You don't play in the same way that you teach. For instance, you teach that the fingers should be kept in such a position, that the wrist should be at a certain level, that the elbows and the shoulders should be this way or the other; and then, when you play, you don't obey any of your rules." Guerrero had apparently pondered over this remark for many, many years, because he realized the truth of it and yet he could never find an explanation. He would say, "I wonder whether the hundreds of things that we consider our duty to submit the student to are not in the way of the final purpose of making music at the piano." He would then enlarge on this discrepancy between performance and technique and quote Franz Liszt who taught that octaves should be played form the wrists, lifting the hand in an exaggerated way and throwing it to the keys, but in performance, was always described as "shaking the octaves out of his sleeve." Again, Liszt always told his students to produce the tone with a vigorous thrusting movement of the forearm, but, Guerrero would say, contemporary descriptions of Liszt's playing were that "his hands came and went, kneading the ebony and ivory of the keyboard."

"The hand is part of the mind" was one of his favourite expressions. He never ceased to be amazed at the miraculous delicacy of hand movements. One of his favourite experiments was to put small objects of different shape and weight on a table and ask a student to lift each object a few inches from the table and put it back in the same place. In this way he would demonstrate the uncanny accuracy and judgment of the amount of power necessary to lift each object which was displayed by the hands. He then elaborated on this demonstration by telling the student that the position of the hand and fingers in this test corresponds exactly to what he would like to see when they were at the piano—that is, with each object having a different shape, the position is different for each one. All this led to his constant emphasis that the discrepancy between technique and performance comes from too much stress being laid on the analysis of the act of playing and not enough thought being given to the integration of all the many movements–"the hand is part of the mind."

He never tired of quoting Mersenne who stated that the art, science, and industry of the hand are so great that the hand may be called one of the principal instruments of wisdom and of reason. Another axiom to which I often heard Guerrero refer was from the ancient Greek, and this was the opinion that "human wisdom resides in the hand, although human beings should be considered wise not merely because they have hands, but rather have they been given hands because they are supposed to be wise. In this way can they execute the dictates of art and reason."

I have never known any teacher of anything who inspired such respect and affection as did Guerrero among his students. They, one and all, adored him. He is irreplaceable, but, although he has gone from us, his work will live on in the enormously talented crowd of students that he has left behind him. There are not many people who can dispose of such a legacy at their passing.

NOTE: This obituary originally appeared in the Royal Conservatory of Music's *Monthly Bulletin* (January–February 1960): 1–2.

appendix 3

Reunion: Participants

Attendees (colleagues, family, friends, former pupils) at the one-day symposium "Remembering Alberto Guerrero," University of Toronto Faculty of Music, 25 October 1990

William Aide, Toronto
Michael Alexander, Toronto
Shirley Pethes Aliferis, West Wester PA
John Beckwith, Toronto
Patricia L'Heureux Bellingham,
    Willimantic CT
Mia Benninga, Toronto
Boris Berlin, Toronto
Helmut Blume, Montreal
Douglas Bodle, Toronto
Alex Champoux, Lennoxville QC
Kathryn Dean, Winnipeg
Mary Wilson Dell, Waterford ON
Victor Dell, Waterford ON
Lois Russell DeVal, Toronto
Gwendolyn Duchemin, Toronto
Fran Dudley, Columbia SC
Ray Dudley, Columbia SC
Marjorie White Francoz, Toronto
Gerry Grace, Toronto

Myrtle Rose Guerrero, Oakville ON
Stuart Hamilton, Toronto
Paul Helmer, Montreal
Ruth Watson Henderson, Toronto
Helen Holman, Charlottetown
Sylvia Hunter, Guelph ON
Cecilia Anderson Ignatieff, Toronto
Mélisande Guerrero Irvine, Toronto
Rosa Arzú Jauer, Toronto
Joyce MacKay Johnson, Toronto
John Jull, Lindsay ON
Edward Laufer, Brampton ON
Nell Trapp Lawson, Toronto
Vera Leinvebers, Toronto
R. Douglas Lloyd, Toronto
Jean Lyons, Vancouver
Gildas McDonald, Toronto
Bruce Mather, Montreal
Pierrette LePage Mather, Montreal
John McIntyre, Mission Hills KS

Kathleen McMorrow, Toronto

Loretto Doherty Miller, Mississauga ON

Elizabeth Baillie Milward, Toronto

Oskar Morawetz, Toronto

Elizabeth Bonnell McCuaig Newton, Prescott ON

Noreen Spencer Nimmons, Thornhill ON

Arthur Ozolins, Toronto

Doreen Miller Pemberton, Toronto

Shaya Petroff, Toronto

Colleen Sadler Pohran, Fonthill ON

Wilfred Powell, Toronto

Guy Purser, Toronto

Jo-Ann Fowler Ras, Toronto

George Ross, Spokane WA

Douglas Scott, Caledonia ON

Margaret Stead Taylor, Ottawa

Oleg Telizyn, Burlington ON

Pearl Kennedy Tory, Toronto

Anne Wolfe Weiser, Ottawa

Former colleagues and students invited to the symposium who were unable to attend. Those who replied in writing are marked.*

Gloria Ackerman, Cincinnati OH

Anahid Alexanian, Erevan, Armenia

Jeanne Grimm Baldy, West St. Paul MN

Ralph Clinch, Saint John NB*

Victor Cox, Brantford ON

Adele Berlin Crone, Mississauga ON

Edward Dorfman, Orillia ON

Shirley Saul Drager, Lougheed AB*

Nancy Boyd Drake, Redmond WA

Margot Rowland Ehling, Vancouver

Robert Finch, Toronto*

Pat Francis Finlay, Sunnyvale CA*

Suzanne Welsh Gibson-Coulthard, Sidney BC*

Dorothy Sandler Glick, Toronto

Shirley Ross Goldsmith, Toronto

Lawrence Goodwill, Stoney Creek ON

Pat Goss, Toronto*

Patricia Rolston Hepner, Richmond BC

Bernice Hoffinger, Toronto*

Janet Horton Kilburn, Beaconsfield QC*

Patricia Perrin Krueger, Toronto

Gordana Lazarevich, Victoria*

Marjorie Lea, Toronto

Eldon Lehman, Toronto

Harold Lugsdin, Winnipeg*

Madeleine Anglin Mackay, Toronto

Florence Dahl Mahon, Calgary*

Ursula Malkin, Vancouver

Denise Mara, Vancouver

Alexandra McGavin, Victoria

Phyllis Runge McIntyre, Windsor ON

Gordon McLean, Victoria*

Anne Altenburg Moot, Kenmore NY*

Laurence Morton, Greenville SC*

Jaroslav Mracek, San Diego CA

Janice Neilson, Toronto*

Irene Brewer Pearce, Hamilton

Freda Coodin Posner, Winnipeg*

Margaret Sheppard Privitello, Thorn-wood NY*

R. Murray Schafer, Indian River ON*

Harvey Silver, Toronto

Malcolm Troup, London UK*

Aube Tzerko, Los Angeles CA

Neil van Allan, St. John's NF

Sondra Verity, Toronto

Alan Walker, Hamilton*

appendix 4

*Excerpts from the Program Note for the Symposium
"Remembering Alberto Guerrero," Toronto,
25 October 1990 (by John Beckwith)*

This symposium celebrates a great teacher whose work deeply influenced a couple of generations of Canadian musicians—pianists for the most part, but teachers, scholars, administrators, and composers as well…

Why has such attention not been paid to his career and influence before now? and indeed why now? The second question is easier than the first. Rather than wait for a suitable multiple of ten in the years since Guerrero's birth or death, the symposium organizers (chiefly Sylvia Hunter and William Aide) felt it was appropriate to invite as many living Guerrero alumni as possible to recall their association with him, for the very reason that such an event had never before taken place. So, back to question number one.

In 1956 Ray Dudley and I tried to assemble a program to mark Guerrero's seventieth birthday. We wanted it to be a surprise for him, but when we were a certain distance along in our planning we brought Myrtle Rose Guerrero in on the secret and her reaction was one of horror: on no account would he want such a tribute, she said, and she persuaded us to cancel the idea. To him a tribute, I guess, smacked of some sort of bandwagon, and he mistrusted bandwagons. Moreover, though passionately serious about his work, he viewed any documenting of *himself* as unimportant…I can reflect now that his attitude exemplifies profoundly his teachings on integrity, authenticity, and genuineness.…

Students, in reminiscing about Guerrero, have often agreed on the strong impact of his intellectual and artistic breadth. It was an extraordinary and powerful experience for young, and more or less provincial, Canadians. I feel fortunate that in my own student days he was still an active performer. Whether in public or at a lesson, his refined and meaningful playing of a wide range of repertoire—from classical structures like the *Appassionata,* the *Italian Concerto,* or Schumann's Opus 17 Fantasy to smaller and more sensuous delights like *Feux d'artifice* or *La maja y el ruiseñor*—made truly admirable models, finely coordinating technical mastery with communicativeness.

With Guerrero, the piano plugged you into music, music plugged you into all the other arts, and altogether they plugged you into life. It was a gestalt. I nodded agreement when a contemporary in his class, my friend Margaret Sheppard Privitello, recently wrote that Guerrero was, as she put it, "one of the strongest forces in my life." He has been that for many of us, I believe, and the symposium may help explore why this is so. And such probing, as distinct from mere platitudes of tribute that he mistrusted, may be more possible at this distance than when he was still with us.

notes

Introduction

1 Helmut Kallmann and Gilles Potvin, eds. *Encyclopedia of Music in Canada*. 2nd ed. (Toronto: University of Toronto Press, 1992), s.v. "Guerrero, Alberto," 559.

2 Emilio Casares Rodicio, ed. *Diccionario de la música española e hispanoamericana* (Madrid: Sociedad General de Autores y Editores, 1999), s.v. "García Guerrero, Alberto," 5: 455–56.

3 Daniel Quiroga, "Los hermanos García Guerrero," *Revista musical chilena* (no. 2, May 1946): 7–13.

4 Personal communication, 28 November 2003.

5 Boyd Neel, "Alberto Guerrero," Royal Conservatory of Music *Monthly Bulletin* (January–February 1960). The Guerrero entry in the online *Encyclopedia of Music in Canada*—http://www.thecanadianencyclopedia.com was corrected and updated in 2004 by me.

6 William Littler, "Remembering Man Who Taught Glenn Gould," *Toronto Star*, 20 October 1990.

7 John Beckwith, "Alberto Guerrero, 1886–1959," *Canadian Music Journal* 4, no. 2 (winter 1960): 33–35; "The Great Piano Teachers: Alberto Guerrero, 1886-1959," *Piano* 9, no. 4 (July/August 2001): 25.

8 Stanley Sadie, ed. *The New Grove Dictionary of Music and Musicians*, 2nd ed. http://www.grovemusic.com (accessed, February 2004).

Chapter One

1 Northrop Frye, *The Bush Garden: Essays on the Canadian Imagination*, 2nd ed. (Toronto: House of Anansi Press, 1995).

2 Mélisande Irvine, interview, 24 April 2002.

3 Gabriel Cobo Contreras, *La Serena: Imagenes de su historia* (La Serena: the author, 1994), 24–25.

4 The historian Pedro Alvarez believes he would have attended the Instituto San Bartolomé, a technical institute in La Serena; the Escuela de Minas in Copiapó was founded only later, around 1870. Personal communication, 9 February 2004.

5   Mélisande Irvine, interview 12 May 2003.

6   These and other details: personal communications, Linda Escobar and Pedro Alvarez, November 2003 through February 2004.

7   Guerrero was educated "without teachers of any kind" and "had no instructors either at the Conservatory of music or privately." Emilio Uzcátegui García, *Músicos chilenos contemporáneos: Datos biográficos e impresiones sobre sus obres* (Santiago: Imprento y Encuardernación América, 1919), 89–90. Regarding Eduardo, Alberto's older brother, Daniel Quiroga claims that "although following no program of the Conservatorio Nacional, he and his brothers are examples of musical autodidacts whose skills were mastered day by day through constant study" ("Los hermanos García Guerrero," 9).

8   Sylvia Hunter, interview, 7 November 2003.

9   Quiroga, "Los hermanos," 9.

10 Kenneth Winters, personal communication, 29 May 2002.

11 Mélisande Irvine, interview, 24 April 2002.

12 Kevin Bazzana, personal communication, 24 July 2003. The notion seems to have originated in a remark of Guerrero to his student George Ross, which Ross relayed to Sylvia Hunter.

13 Alberto's older brother, Carlos, graduated from the Liceo de Hombres in 1892. (Pedro Alvarez, personal communication, 22 January 2004).

14 Ibid.

15 This was the recollection of both Margaret Sheppard Privitello and Ray Dudley, from their studies with Guerrero. In a conversation remembered by William Aide, Guerrero said only that his family had wanted him to become a priest.

16 *Diario El Coquimbo*, La Serena, 24 September 1892. The Arqueros silver mine was discovered in 1825 (see Cobo Contreras, *La Serena*, 23–24).

17 Vicente Salas Viú, *La Creación musical en Chile, 1900–1951* (Santiago: Ediciones de la Universidad de Chile, n.d. [1952?]), 30. Casares Rodicio, *Diccionario*, 5: 455.

18 Instituto Nacional de Chile, examination records, 1900 and 1901, obtained through the kind assistance of Graciela Muñoz, April 2004.

19 William Belmont Parker, "Alberto García Guerrero," *Chileans of Today* (Santiago: Hispanic Society of America 1920; New York: Kraus, 1967), 391.

20 A certificate of the Ministerio de Educación, dated 16 August 2005, obtained with the help of Nieves Carrasco, verifies that Guerrero was a student at the Instituto Nacional in 1900 and 1901, and at the Internado Barros Arana in 1902 and 1903. There is no record of where (or whether) he completed the usual fifth and sixth years of the "humanidades" program.

21 Quiroga, "Los hermanos," 12. The specific writers' names mentioned suggest that, despite his later identification with French musical taste, he was aware of both French and German contemporary approaches in music theory.

22 The present owner of this collection, David Finch, kindly provided a list of the contents.

23 Virgilio Figueroa, *Diccionario histórico, biográfico y bibliográfico de Chile* (Santiago: the author, 1928; Nendeln/Liechtenstein: Kraus, 1974), 3: 288.

24 Fernando García Arancibia, interview, 21 January 2003.

25 From clippings preserved in the Guerrero Collection, Faculty of Music library, University of Toronto.

26 Ibid.

27 Daniel Quiroga summarizes the lectures on Schumann and Wagner in "Los hermanos" (10). No doubt Alberto's piano illustrations for Wagner relied on the piano transcriptions by Liszt. No specific mention is made about his illustrations for Paganini, necessarily also transcriptions (there is no solo piano music by Niccolò Paganini). Edward MacDowell (d. 1908), then at a peak of posthumous popularity, stands out as the only New World composer in the list; it is not known which of his works were chosen for illustration.

28 Stanley Sadie, *The New Grove Dictionary of Opera* (London: Macmillan, 1992), 4: 172–73. Pablo Gonzalez, cited in Esteban Cabezas, "El pianista desconocido," *El Mercurio*, 24 November 2002.

29 *El Mercurio*, 3 July 1914

30 *El Mercurio*, 9 July 1914

31 Cited in Luis Merino Montero, "Neuvas luces sobre Acario Cotapos," *Revista musical chilena* no. 159 (January–June 1983): 9.

32 Carvajal was evidently not related to Nicolasa Guerrero Carvajal, Guerrero's mother. When a permanent orchestra was eventually established in Santiago, in the 1930s, he became its conductor.

33 Uzcátegui, *Músicos Chilenos*, chapter 4, "Armando Carvajal."

34 The three "trios concertants" of Franck's Opus 1 do not include a work in E; Robin Elliott points out that the piano-trio arrangement by Henry Woollett of Franck's Prélude, Aria, and Finale is in this key; but the program listing may be an error.

35 Alfonso Leng, "El distinguido compositor y pianista chileno Dn. Alberto García Guerrero," *Música* 2, no. 2 (March 1921): 1–2.

36 Samuel Claro Valdés, *Rosita Renard, pianista chilena* (Santiago: A. Bello, 1993), 38.

37 Three works by Guerrero appear in the numbered catalogue: *Chants oubliés*, N.2.26; *Capricho*, N.9.1.144; *Vals triste*, N.9.1.145, ed. Roberto Escobar and Renato Yrarrázaval (*Música Compuesta en Chile*, 1900–68 [Santiago: Ediciones de la Biblioteca Nacional, 1969]).

38 Hans Lach, review, *Los Diez*, 9, 1917.

39 The manuscripts are preserved in the Guerrero Collection, Faculty of Music library, University of Toronto. *Vals triste* appeared in *Los Diez*, no. 9 (1917): 12–13, retitled in French, "Valse triste." The manuscript of *To Maud Allan* was reproduced in *Los Diez*, no. 3 (1916), and again in Uzcátegui García, *Músicos chilenos*, 99. The manuscript's "Allan" is sometimes reproduced as "Allen."

40 As late as 1929, Domingo Santa Cruz was bemoaning the Italian domination of Chilean operatic life in an article called "Los funerales de la ópera" in *El Mercurio* (cited in Mario Cánepo Guzmán, *La ópera en Chile 1839–1930* [Santiago: Editorial del Pacifico, 1976], 270, and also by Robert Stevenson in Sadie, *New Grove Dictionary of Opera*).

41 Guzmán 1976

42 Aurelio Díaz Meza (1879–1933) was a "journalist, historian, playwright, theatre critic, and entrepreneur...known for his collections of Chilean legends and traditions...[His] career as a playwright began in 1908 when *Rucacahuiñ*, a zarzuela... with music by Alberto García, premiered," (Eladio Cortés and Mirta Barrea-Marlys, *Encyclopedia of Latin American Theater* [Westport, CT: Greenwood Press, 2003], 110–11). For further biographical details, and a list of publications, see Biblioteca Ayacucho, *Diccionario enciclopedico de las letras de América latina* (Caracas: Monte Avila Editores, 1995), 1483.

43 Díaz Meza 1914; *Mundo Teatral* 1, no. 3 (December 1918): 24–32.

44 *El Diario ilustrado*, 24 July 1908.

45 *El Mercurio*, 6 August 1908.

46 "The sentimental *romanza* sung by Pilar García roused the public to great applause, and was encored" (*El Diario ilustrado*, 24 July 1908).

47 Excerpts from Vézina's score are found in *The Canadian Musical Heritage / Le patrimoine musical canadien*, vol. 10 ("Opera and operetta excerpts 1"), edited by Dorith R. Cooper, Ottawa: Canadian Musical Heritage Society, 1991, 180–202.

48 Alberto Guerrero, "Un compositor ignorado," *Negro y blanco* 1, no. 1 (December 1911): 5. Referring to Leng as "an intuitive musician," Guerrero comments on various of his scores, including the piano piece *Doloras*, a piano sonata, and a Romanza for violin and piano.

49 Luis Merino Montero, "Neuvas luces," 11–12

50 For example, Figueroa, *Diccionario histórico* (1928), 288; see also Quiroga, "Los hermanos," 8.

51 Julio Ramírez Cádiz, dean, Faculty of Dentistry, Universidad de Chile, personal communication, 5 November 2003.

52 Anon. (Leng?), "Alberto García Guerrero, 1886–1959," *Revista musical chilena*, no. 68 (November/December 1959): 130.

53 Eugenio Pereira Salas, "La música chilena en los primeros cinquenta años del siglo XX," *Revista musical chilena*, no. 40 (Summer 1950–51): 66–67.

54 Quiroga, "Los Hermanos," 9.

55 Ibid., 9.

56 Casares Rodicio, *Diccionario*.

57 Samuel Claro Valdés and Jorge Urrutia Bondel, *Historia de la Música en Chile* (Santiago: Editorial Orbe, 1973), 123.

58 Valerio Maino Prado et al., eds., *Los Diez en el arte chileno del siglo XX* (Santiago: 1976). Domingo Santa Cruz mentions two other artists associated with the group: the playwright Eduardo Barrios and the author-critic Augusto D'Halmar ("Mis recuerdos sobre la sociedad Bach," *Revista musical chilena*, no. 40 (Spring 1950–51): 55n. Another writer, Ernest A. Guzmán, is also cited. The members "came together… based on their affinity of 'crossing over' and complementing artistic pursuits of different disciplines…[Their] trademark 'X,' also used to identify their literary productions, conveys the interdisciplinary 'crossing over' and alludes to the unknown, accepted by its members as the group began to take shape in an atmosphere of enigmatic humor." (Ricardo Loebell, "Julio Bertrand y Los Diez—X" in *La Mirada Ricobrada* by Julio Bertrand Vidal [Santiago: Morgan Impresores 2004], 155). *La muerte de Alsino* is available on the CD *Bicentenario de la Música Sinfónica de Chile, vol. 1* (Academia Chilena de Bellas Artes ABA-SVR 7000-1, 2003), along with works by Soro and Santa Cruz.

59 Merino Montero, "Neuvas luces," 9.

60 Santa Cruz,"Mis recuerdos," 9–12.

61 Ibid., 10

62 Ibid., 11–12. Of Arnold Schoenberg's four string quartets, only nos. 1 and 2 had been composed at this date.

63 Marta Canales Pizarro (1893–1986) became a prominent composer and choral conductor in Chile; she and her brothers were among the young participants in the Sociedad Bach chorus.

64 According to Salas Viú, the Sociedad was founded "on the initiative of the García Guerrero brothers" (*La Creacion*, 29). While he may have played a role in planning, in June 1917 Alberto Guerrero was living in New York. He no doubt participated more actively during his return to Chile in the first half of 1918.

65 Santa Cruz, "Mis recuerdos," 12.

66 Alfonso Leng, *Cuatro preludios para piano* (Santiago: Ediciones del Conservatorio Nacional de Música, 1929); copy in the Faculty of Music library, University of Toronto

67 Leng, "Decimo aniversario."

68 Cuevas Mackenna, personal communication, through Jaime Oxley, 11 December 2003; also, Quiroga, personal communication, 18 November 2003.

69 Luigi Stephano Giarda (1868–1952), Italian-born cellist and composer, former first cellist of the La Scala orchestra, Milan, professor of cello playing and theory at the Conservatorio Nacional, Santiago, from 1905.

70 *El Diario ilustrado*, 7 May 1907; other Trio Giarda articles, 14 May 1907 and 28 May 1907.

71 "La Temporada Lirica," "Los artistas de la compañia," *El Diario ilustrado*, 23 July 1907; "El repertorio de la compañia," 5 August 1907 (both front page features). In fact the two Wagner operas had been mounted at the Municipal in the 1890s, and it seems *Lohengrin* was in the repertoire at this time; he was evidently pointing out that the company seemed now unfit for them.

72 Ibid., 20 July 1908, 27 June 1907, 8 October 1908.

73 *El Diario ilustrado*, 10 October 1907; the quotation is from *Hamlet*, act 3, scene 2.

74 Leng, "El distinguido," 1–2.

75 Uzcátegui, *Músicos chilenos*, 93–94.

Chapter Two

1 Virgilio Figueroa, *Diccionario histórico, biográfico y bibliográfico de Chile* (Santiago: the author, 1931), 5: 1093.

2 These and the following quotes concerning the tour are all from clippings and programs in the Guerrero Collection, Faculty of Music library, University of Toronto.

3 Alfonso Leng, "Dos notables artistas," source unknown (clipping in the Guerrero Collection, Faculty of Music library, University of Toronto). The article includes a photo of Penha and Guerrero.

4 Clipping, undated and untitled, Faculty of Music library, U of T.

5 Leng, "Dos notables."

6 There is no composition by Robert Schumann with this title. The Five Pieces, Opus 102, do not have individual titles. Was it a cello and piano arrangement of the well-known *Träumerei* from his Opus 15?

7 Ray Dudley, "Alberto Guerrero and Glenn Gould: My View," *New Journal for Music* 1, no. 1 (Summer 1990); also, personal communication, n.d. (2003).

8 Kathleen McMorrow discovered this item.

9 Alberto Guerrero to the author, 18 January 1951. See page 109.

10 New Orleans *Times-Picayune*, n.d.

11 *Musical Courier*, 19 October 1916.

12 New York *American*, 15 December 1916. The sharing evidently was not a chance occurrence; Ruckert had appeared with Penha in concerts in Chile the previous year.

13 A.H., *Musical America*, 23 December 1916.

14 Thanks to Raffi Kosover for making the translation.

15 Stuart Hamilton, interview, 17 November 2003.

16 *Musical courier*, 1 June 1916 (Bynner Papers, Houghton Library, Harvard University). The Toronto-born interpretive dancer Maud Allan (1878–1956) was internationally known for her performances in *The Vision of Salome*.

17 *El Magallanes*, Punta Arenas, 24 December 1917; 28 December 1917; 23 January 1918. Thanks to Jaime Gómez, Biblioteca Nacional, Santiago, for locating these references.

18 Guerrero Collection, Faculty of Music library, University of Toronto.

19 Luis Merino Montero calls him "one of the first to present Schoenberg's music in Chile." "Cinco efemérides en la creación musical chilena," *Revista musical chilena*, no. 167 (January/June 1987): 45. Vicente Salas Viú specifies Opus 11 as having been performed by him (*La Creación musical en Chile, 1900–1951* [Santiago: Ediciones de la Universidad de Chile, n.d.]).

20 Emilio Uzcátegui García, *Músicos chilenos contemporáneos*, 93.

21 *El Mercurio*, 1 June 1918. Some of the Debussy pieces performed were published less than a decade previously.

22 Uzcátegui, *Músicos chilenos*, 95.

23 *El Mercurio*, 28 June 1918.

24 Ibid. The reviewer's only criticisms are directed to the weakness of certain sections of the ad-hoc orchestra, signalling a then still unsolved problem in Santiago's musical life.

25 Uzcátegui, *Músicos chilenos*.

26 The letter is in the Guerrero Collection, Faculty of Music library, University of Toronto.

27 Personal communication, 18 March 2004. Dudley says Guerrero "was always trying to discourage this direction in my life and no matter how awful he would describe being a concert pianist, I always would say at the next lesson—*I still wanted to be a concert pianist*" (personal communication, 27 February 2004).

Chapter Three

1 Eric Koch, *The Brothers Hambourg* (Toronto: Robin Brass, 1997). See also Helmut Kallmann and Gilles Potvin, eds., "Hambourg," "Hambourg Conservatory of Music," *Encyclopedia of Music in Canada*, 2nd ed. (Toronto: University of Toronto Press, 1992).

2 Bernard Preston, "Famous Musician Arrives in Toronto," Toronto *Sunday World*, 28 August 1918.

3 Ibid.

4 Undated clippings, Guerrero Collection.

5 Undated clipping, Guerrero Collection. Biographies of Moore claim that he had returned to England by this time, but the documents clearly indicate that he was in Toronto, active as a performer there, and a student of Guerrero's, at least during 1918–19, and possibly longer.

6 Unidentified review, Guerrero Collection, Faculty of Music library, University of Toronto.

7 The *Free Press*; the *Advertiser*, 23 January 1919. From Guerrero Collection, Faculty of Music Library, University of Toronto.

8 New York review by Max Smith. Undated clipping (6 January 1920?), Guerrero Collection.

9 Shortly after settling in Canada, in December 1919, Campbell-McInnes was Guerrero's "associate artist" in a recital in London, Ontario, *Canadian Journal of Music* 6, no. 3 (December 1919): 46.

10 Manelik [pseud.], "Un artista chilena en Norteamérica," *El Mercurio*, 31 October 1920. (This pseudonym has been identified with Guerrero's librettist-partner, Aurelio Díaz Meza.) See also Alfonso Leng, "El distinguido compositor y pianista chileno Dn. Alberto García Guerrero," *Música* 2, no. 3 (March 1921): 1–2.

11 *El Mercurio*, 21 March 1919.

12 Virgilio Figueroa, *Diccionario histórico, biográfico y bibliográfico de Chile*, s.v. "García Guerrero, Alberto; García Guerrero, Eduardo," 3: 289.

13 Czaplinski remained with the group for less than two seasons: see Koch, *The Brothers Hambourg*, 136–40. The original Hambourg Trio (Mark, Jan, and Boris) reunited briefly in 1935 for a cross-Canada tour, including a performance of Beethoven's *Triple Concerto* with the TSO (Koch, x and 187–88).

14 "A Picturesque Programme," n.p., n.d., from the Guerrero Collection.

15 Carol Oja, *Colin McPhee, Composer in Two Worlds* (Washington: Smithsonian Institution Press, 1990), 17.

16 *Musical Canada* 6, no. 5 (May 1925): 19–20.

17 *Star*, 3 April 1924.

18 *Star*, 19 April 1924.

19 *Radio Evening Public Ledger*, Philadelphia, n.d.

20 *Conservatory Quarterly Review*, 7 February 1925, 61.

21 *Globe*, 29 May 1924.

22 W.O. Forsyth: "Canadian Composers," *Canadian Journal of Music* 2, no. 2 (June 1915): 20–21.

23 Luigi von Kunits, Editorial, "Orchestral Problems: Aims and Ideals," *Canadian Journal of Music* 2, no. 4 (August 1915): 51–53.

24 The documents were obtained with the assistance of Matías Ahumada of the Chilean consulate in Toronto.

25 Carmen G. Duhart, archivist, personal communication, 23 January 2004.

26 "I have not a very good idea of his financial position just now, as he talks very little about it, and never mentions his wife and daughter in Paris, except to show me every now and then a small sheaf of drawings his daughter has done in pencil on odds and ends of paper and sent for his inspection" (Robert Finch to Ian Mackinnon-Pearson, 3 March 1935). Finch Papers, Thomas Fisher Rare Book Library, University of Toronto, box 14, file 15.

27 *El Mercurio* [?], 26 December 1933. The letter and clippings are in the Guerrero Collection.

28 Mélisande Irvine, interview, 24 April 2002.

29 The Royal Conservatory examinations department has not preserved records of the annual tour assignments, and they do not appear among the TCM papers in the University of Toronto Archives.

30 Saskatoon *Star-Phoenix*, 7 July 1931; "The successful enrolment for the course in piano technique and interpretation given in the city by Señor Guerrero during the past week, is an encouraging sign."—K.U., "Musical Notes," *Edmonton Journal*, 9 July 1932.

31 Toronto Conservatory of Music papers, University of Toronto Archives, A1975–0014, box 69 ("Finances, 1920–25"). Payments to teachers were made quarterly. For the first two seasons of Guerrero's contract, records are incomplete.

32 Ibid., boxes 7 through 10 ("Year book, 1923–61").

33 Guerrero, "Promenade," *Conservatory Quarterly Review* 14, no. 2 (Winter 1932): 43.

34 TCM papers, box 40 ("Summer School prospectus, 1937–47").

35 "The keynote…was sound musicianship, not sensationalism, so that this great work was impressive in the way intended by its composer," Lawrence Mason, *Globe*, 20 February 1935.

36 Thanks to David Finch, executor of the estate of Myrtle Rose Guerrero, for discovering this item. The inscription is signed, "Love, Melisande," and there are two words crossed out, making the original read "will collaborate with him *as composer.*" Mélisande Irvine has forgotten the episode, and whether she had young ambitions to be a composer (interview, 25 August 2003). A more plausible interpretation is suggested by Robin Elliott: since Stravinsky's son Theodore was the illustrator of the *Jeu de cartes* score, Guerrero's daughter looked forward to one day illustrating one of *his* compositions.

37 J. Gordon Andison, letter to Carl Morey, 29 December 1983, speaks of three performances by Guerrero in the 1930s which impressed him deeply. The first of these ("something I shall never forget") is the *Petrushka* arrangement, in Eaton Auditorium in 1932; the other two are the Brahms Second Concerto with the TSO in 1935 and the J.S. Bach *Goldberg Variations* at the TCM in 1937 (quoted by permission of Carl Morey).

38 *Saturday Night*, 17 December 1932.

Chapter Four

1 *Saturday Night*, 4 April 1936; see also Carl Morey, "The Beginnings of Modernism in Toronto," in *Célébration: Essays on Aspects of Canadian Music*, ed. Godfrey Ridout and Talivaldis Kenins (Toronto: Canadian Music Centre, 1984), 83.

2 J. Gordon Andison to Carl Morey, 29 December 1983.

3 Toronto Reference Library program files ("Guerrero, Alberto"); reviews, *Saturday Night*; Finch Papers, Thomas Fisher Rare Books Library, University of Toronto, box 25, files 15, 20.

4 Finch Papers, box 14, file 15.

5 *Saturday Night*, 15 December 1934; no precise identification of program items is given.

6 *Saturday Night*, 4 April 1936; no precise identification of program items.

7 Finch Papers, box 14, file 15.

8 Toronto Reference Library program files.

9 The first two volumes in the series were *Seize sonates anciennes d'auteurs espagnols*, Paris 1925, and *Dix-sept sonates et pièces d'auteurs espagnols* (Paris: M. Eschig, 1929). Guerrero appears to have acquired them soon after publication.

10 Guerrero repeated the Inventions recital in the Friday afternoon series at Hart House on 29 November 1935.

11 *Saturday Night*, 10 November 1934; 30 November 1935; 15 May 1937.

12 Finch Papers, box 14, file 15.

13 The Murch family consisted of four brothers: Edward, a singer; Walter, an artist; Frank, and Louis, both pianists who studied with Guerrero. Frank also had some experience as a conductor, and was later active in Ann Arbor, Michigan. Their mother, Louise Murch (*née* Tandy), taught voice and piano in Toronto where she died at the advanced age of 100. Thanks to Anna and William McCoy, for clarification, December 2003.

14 The reference is puzzling; no Mozart sonata appears on the program of this recital.

15 Guerrero was an advocate of electric hand massage as a replacement for mechanical exercises at the keyboard.

16 Guerrero's contributions were the Chopin Barcarolle and Dohnanyi's *Naila* Waltz.

17 Location of this sketch is unknown.

18 Norman Wilks (1885–1944), a member of the TCM piano faculty from 1928, later vice-principal and, 1942–44, principal.

19 Harold Samuel (1879–1937), the English pianist, was noted as a Bach specialist. He toured Canada several times as a recitalist and also as a festival adjudicator.

20 Mrs. H is unidentified.

21 Duncan was an important Toronto art dealer, proprietor of the Picture Loan Society. Daniells, like Finch a published poet, was with the University College English department. Lange was a noted German scholar. Jarvis later became a well-known art critic.

22 Étienne Gilson (1884–1978), French philosopher, founded the Pontifical Institute of Medieval Studies at St. Michael's College, University of Toronto.

23 Myrtle Rose and Alberto Guerrero: *The New Approach to the Piano:* or, how to teach beginners in a manner both agreeable and instructive, individually as well as in groups, and containing not only the first pieces to be used in teaching but also how to teach them; part 1 (Oakville, ON: Frederick Harris, 1935); part 2, 1936.

24 Saskatoon *Star-Phoenix*, 7 July 1931.

25 Alberto Guerrero. *Tango* (Oakville, ON: Frederick Harris, 1937). Publisher's proofs, and orchestral arrangements, Guerrero Collection, Faculty of Music library, University of Toronto. *Southern Seas: Petite Valse*, Oakville, Ontario, 1937. The *Tango* was reprinted in *Souvenir Album: A History of the Frederick Harris Music Co. Ltd., 1904–1984* (Oakville, ON: Frederick Harris, 1984).

26 *Saturday Night*, 7 May 1927.

27 Fred Jacob, *Mail and Empire*, 3 November 1927.

28 *Saturday Night*, 16 March 1929.

29 *Conservatory Quarterly Review*, no. 11 (Winter 1929): 72–73.

30 Paul Helmer discovered this document in the National Archives, Ottawa, and kindly relayed the details.

31 Most of this information came from an interview with Mélisande Irvine, 25 August 2003.

32 Margaret Sheppard Privitello, personal communication, 19 December 2002.

33 Adolph Koldofsky (1905–51) was the second violinist in the Hart House String Quartet, and an orchestral player and conductor in Toronto, later moving to Vancouver and eventually Los Angeles, where he played in the premières of Schoenberg's String Trio and Fantasy. The latter work is dedicated to him.

34 Alberto Guerrero, letter to Margaret Sheppard, 10 August [194?].

35 Privitello, personal communication, 2 February 1997.

36 Neither the church archives nor the Peaker Collection at the National Library of Canada's music division could verify such a program. A likely date would be 1947 or '48.

37 Daniel Quiroga, "Los hermanos García Guerrero," *Revista musical chilena* vol. 2 (May 1946): 7–13.

38 TCM papers, University of Toronto Archives, A-1975–0014, box 108 ("biographies, Ge-Hal").

Chapter Five

1 Margaret Sheppard Privitello, personal communication, October 1990.
2 This quotation has not been traced.
3 Mélisande Irvine interview, 12 May 2003.
4 William Aide, *Starting from Porcupine* (Ottawa: Oberon, 1996), 35.
5 Ibid., 34
6 Ibid., 30
7 John Beckwith, "The Great Piano Teachers: Alberto Guerrero, 1886–1959." *Piano* 9, no. 4 (July–August 2001): 25.
8 TCM papers, University of Toronto Archives, A1975-0014, box 108 (Guerrero file).
9 Alexis Carrel, *L'homme, cet inconnu*, Paris: Librairie Plon, 1935; English translation, *Man the Unknown* (New York: Harper and Brothers, 1935).
10 He had been knighted in 1935, one of the last knighthoods awarded in Canada, and the only one to a musician. Guerrero thought he was too young for the honour.
11 Edith Borroff explores this historical phenomenon as experienced by American composers of the period in her book called *Three American Composers* (Lanhan, MD: University Press of America, 1986), 4–10.
12 James Endicott (1865–1954), former moderator of the United Church of Canada, was father to both Professor Norman Endicott and the Reverend James Gareth Endicott, noted China missionary and communist activist.
13 According to the Ontario death registration, she died on 14 June 1950, aged 20 days.
14 Michel Schneider, *Glenn Gould, piano solo*, Paris: Gallimard, 1988 and 1994, 22.
15 Aide, *Starting from Porcupine*; Kevin Bazzana, *Wondrous Strange: The Life and Art of Glenn Gould* (Toronto: McClelland and Stewart, 2003).
16 Margaret Sheppard Privitello, personal communication, 2 February 1997.
17 Glenn Gould, interview with Martin Mayer, cited in Otto Friedrich, *Glenn Gould: A Life and Variations* (Toronto: Lester and Orpen Dennys, 1989), 51.
18 Aide, *Starting from Porcupine*, 31–33.
19 Jock Carroll, *Glenn Gould: Some Portraits of the Artist as a Young Man* (Toronto: Stoddard, 1995), 76; see also John Beckwith, "Glenn Gould, the Early Years: Addenda and Corrigenda," *GlennGould* 2, no. 2 (Fall 1996): 59.
20 Otto Ortmann, *The Physiological Mechanics of Piano Technique* (London: E.P. Dutton, 1929). See chapters 17 and 20.
21 Ruth Watson Henderson, personal communication, 23 February 2004.
22 Mary Wilson Dell, personal communication, 2 March 2004. For further comments on the technique, see Aide, *Starting from Porcupine*, 32–33, and John Beckwith, "Shattering a Few Myths" in *Music Papers: Articles and Talks by a Canadian Composer, 1961–1994* (Ottawa: Golden Dog, 1997), 170.
23 Ray Dudley, "Alberto Guerrero and Glenn Gould: My View," *New Journal for Music* 1, no. 1 (Summer 1990): 65–99; quoted in Beckwith, "Glenn Gould, the early years," 60–61.
24 Ibid.; also, Bazzana, *Wondrous Strange*, 68.
25 Pierrette LePage, personal communication, 22 February 2004.
26 Robert J. Silverman, "Claudio Arrau, an Interview," *Piano Quarterly* 31, no. 120 (1982): 30–33.
27 Stuart Hamilton, quoted in Beckwith, "Glenn Gould, the early years," 63; also, interview, 17 November 2003.
28 Edward W. Said: "Music as an Extreme Occasion," in his *Musical Elaborations* (New York: Columbia University Press, 1991), 22.

29 Alex Champoux, personal communication, 16 March 2004.

30 Cited in Otto Friedrich, *Glenn Gould*, 16.

31 Kenneth Winters, CBC Radio documentary, "Five Great Music Teachers," 5 November 1996.

32 Beckwith, "Glenn Gould, the early years," 63. Sylvia Hunter, personal communication, 22 June 1997. In 2004, the LP was rereleased as a compact disc, VAI Audio CD 1198, with no corrections to the identifying notes. Thanks to Kevin Bazzana for alerting me to this.

33 Sylvia Hunter, personal communication, 22 June 1997; interview, 7 November 2003.

34 Ray Dudley, interview, 17 February 2004; Arthur Ozolins, interview by Kenneth Winters, CBC Radio, 5 November 1996; Pierrette LePage, personal communication, 22 February 2004.

35 Original in the Faculty of Music library, University of Toronto, special collections.

36 Nadia Boulanger, my composition teacher.

37 The American composer Aaron Copland was a guest speaker at the Royal Conservatory's convocation. Ettore Mazzoleni was the conservatory principal.

38 Godfrey Ridout (1920–86), composer and teacher.

39 The Canadian composer who studied with Milhaud was Murray Adaskin (1906–2000).

40 Glenn Gould's concert in the Royal Conservatory Concert Hall, 4 January 1951, included Ernst Krenek's Piano Sonata no. 3 and the première of Gould's own Sonata for bassoon and piano, with Nicholas Kilburn, bassoonist.

41 My wife, Pamela Terry.

42 The friend was probably Michael Penha, the cellist with whom Guerrero performed in his early career.

43 The event was noted briefly in the society columns of the *Star*, 21 November 1952. A year later, the school invited him to give another recital, but he declined, suggesting instead his young pupil, Ruth Watson (Watson Henderson, personal communication, 23 February 2004).

44 Finch Papers, box 14, file 2.

Chapter Six

1 "Iturbi Packs Massey Hall," *Globe and Mail*, 20 April 1951.

2 "Kapell Program at Massey Hall Conservative," *Globe and Mail*, 24 April 1951.

3 Glenn Gould, card to the author, Christmas 1951.

4 R. Murray Schafer, personal communication, 15 July 2002.

5 Robertson Davies, *The Cunning Man* (Toronto: McClelland and Stewart, 1994). See especially 283–88.

6 Robertson Davies, letter to the editor, *Globe and Mail*, 14 October 1995.

7 Myrtle Rose Guerrero, letter to the author, 15 September 1951.

8 Ray Dudley, personal communication, 30 January 2004.

9 Margaret Sheppard Privitello, personal communication, 27 May 1997.

10 Aide, *Starting from Porcupine* (Ottawa: Oberon, 1996), 26, 30.

11 Ibid., 29

12 John Roberts, ed., *The Art of Glenn Gould: Reflections of a Musical Genius* (Toronto: Malcolm Lester, 1999), 138. The interviewer was Alan Rich, and the interview, originally broadcast on KPFA, Berkeley, 25 October 1959, was repeated on CBC Radio, 30 December 1959.

13 A recording is available from CBC Records: *Ovation*, vol. 2, PSCD 2027–5.

14 Boyd Neel, "Alberto Guerrero," Royal Conservatory of Music *Monthly Bulletin* (January–February 1960): 1–2.

15 Boyd Neel, *My Orchestras and Other Adventures: The Memoirs of Boyd Neel*, ed. J. David Finch (Toronto: University of Toronto Press, 1985).

16 Aide, *Starting from Porcupine*, 29.

17 Anon. [Leng?] "Alberto García Guerrero, 1886–1959," *Revista musical chilena* (November–December 1959): 130–31.

18 Aide, *Starting from Porcupine*, 29

19 Bruce Mather, letter to William Aide, 15 September 1990.

20 This episode was related only years later by Myrtle Rose Guerrero, who was present at the late-evening meeting.

21 Program note to R. Murray Schafer, *In Memoriam Alberto Guerrero*, 1959.

22 Aide, *Starting from Porcupine*, 27, 29

23 Laurence Morton, letter to William Aide, 3 October 1990.

24 Sylvia Hunter, personal communication, 15 March 2004.

25 Pierrette LePage, personal communication, 22 February 2004.

26 Edward Laufer, personal communication, 8 April 2004.

27 Ray Dudley, personal communication, 27 February 2004.

28 Mary Wilson Dell, personal communications, 2 February 2004, 30 March 2004.

29 Reissued as VAI Audio CD 1198.

30 His left-hand lines are a reminder, perhaps, of his critical comments on William Kapell's Bach, in 1951.

31 Sylvia Hunter, one of the principal organizers of the event, kindly provided the lists in Appendix 3.

32 Mélisande Irvine, interview with Kevin Bazzana, 2 August 2001.

bibliography

Aide, William. *Starting from Porcupine*. Ottawa: Oberon, 1996.

———. "In loco parentis." *Piano* 9, no. 4 (July–August 2001): 27–29.

Anon. [Alfonso Leng?]. "Alberto García Guerrero, 1886–1959." *Revista musical chilena* no. 68 (November–December 1959): 130–31.

Bazzana, Kevin. *Wondrous Strange: The Life and Art of Glenn Gould*. Toronto: McClelland and Stewart, 2003.

Beckwith, John. "Alberto Guerrero, 1886–1959." *Canadian Music Journal* 4, no. 2 (Winter 1960): 33–35.

———. "Glenn Gould, The Early Years: Addenda and Corrigenda." *Glenn Gould* 2, no. 2 (Fall 1996): 56–65.

———. "The Great Piano Teachers: Alberto Guerrero, 1886–1959." *Piano* 9, no. 4 (July–August 2001): 25.

———. "Remembering Alberto Guerrero." Notes for the Alberto Guerrero Symposium Program. Toronto. 25 October 1990.

———. "Shattering a Few Myths." In *Music Papers: Articles and Talks by a Canadian composer, 1961–1994*, 160–75. Ottawa: Golden Dog Press, 1997.

Béhague, Gerard. *Music in Latin America: An Introduction*. Englewood Cliffs, NJ: Prentice-Hall, 1979.

Biblioteca Ayacucho. *Diccionario enciclopedico de las letras de América latina*. Caracas: Monte Avila Editores Latinoamericana, 1995.

Borroff, Edith. *Three American Composers*. Lanham, MD: University Press of America, 1986.

Cabezas, Esteban. "El pianista desconocido." *El Mercurio*, 24 November 2002.

Carroll, Jock. *Glenn Gould: Some Portraits of the Artist as a Young Man*. Toronto: Stoddard, 1995.

Casares Rodicio, Emilio, ed. *Diccionario de la música española e hispanoamericana*. Vol. 5. Madrid: Sociedad General de Autores y Editores, 1999.

Claro Valdés, Samuel. *Rosita Renard, pianista chilena*. Santiago: A. Bello, 1993.

———. "La Tertulia musical como antecedente de los compositores decimales." In *Los Diez en el arte chileno del siglo XX*, ed. Valeria Maino Prado et al., 39–49. Santiago: Editorial Universitaria, 1976.

Claro Valdés, Samuel, and Jorge Urrutia Bondel. *Historia de la Música en Chile.* Santiago: Editorial Orbe, 1973.

Cobo Contreras, Gabriel. *La Serena: Imagenes de su historia.* La Serena: the author, 1994.

Cortés, Eladio, and Mirta Barrea-Marlys. *Encyclopedia of Latin American Theater.* Westport, CT: Greenwood, 2003.

Dudley, Ray. "Alberto Guerrero and Glenn Gould: My View." *New Journal for Music* 1, no. 1 (Summer 1990): 65–99.

Escobar, Roberto, and Renato Yrarrázaval, eds. *Música compuesta en Chile, 1900–68.* Santiago: Ediciones de la Biblioteca Nacional, 1969.

Figueroa, Virgilio. *Diccionario histórico, biográfico y bibliográfico de Chile.* Santiago: the author, 1925–31. Reprint, Nendeln/Liechtenstein: Kraus-Thomson, 1974. Vols. 3 and 5.

Finch, Robert. Papers. Thomas Fisher Library. University of Toronto.

Finscher, Ludwig, ed. *Die Musik in Geschichte und Gegenwart.* 2nd ed. Kassel: Bärenreiter-Verlag, 1995.

Friedrich, Otto. *Glenn Gould: A Life and Variations.* Toronto: Lester and Orpen Dennys, 1989.

Guerrero, Alberto. "Un compositor ignorado." *Negro y blanco* 1, no. 1 (December 1911): 5.

———. "The Discrepancy between Performance and Technique." Royal Conservatory of Music *Monthly Bulletin,* October 1950, 2–3.

———. "Iturbi Packs Massey Hall." *The Globe and Mail,* 20 April 1951.

———. "Kapell Program at Massey Hall Conventional." *Globe and Mail,* 24 April 1951.

———. Papers. "Guerrero Collection." Rare Books and Special Collections. Faculty of Music Library. University of Toronto.

———. "Promenade." *Conservatory Quarterly Review* 14, no. 2 (Winter 1932): 43.

Guzmán, Mario Cánepa. *La ópera en Chile, 1839–1930.* Santiago: Editorial del Pacifico, 1976.

Kallmann, Helmut, and Gilles Potvin, eds. *Encyclopedia of Music in Canada.* 2nd ed. Toronto: University of Toronto Press, 1992.

Koch, Eric. *The Brothers Hambourg.* Toronto: Robin Brass Studio, 1997.

Leng, Alfonso. "Decimo aniversario de la muerte de tres músicos chilenos [Allende, Bisquertt, García Guerrero]." *Revista musical chilena* no. 107 (April–June 1969): 76.

———. "El distinguido compositor y pianista chileno Dn. Alberto García Guerrero." *Música* 2, no. 3 (March 1921): 1–2.

Loebell, Ricardo. "Julio Bertrand y Los Diez—X." In *La Mirada Ricobrada,* by Julio Bertrand Vidal, 153–63. Santiago: Morgan Impresores, 2004.

Manelik [Aurelio Díaz Meza]. "Un Artista Chilena en Norteamérica." *El Mercurio,* 31 October 1920; reprinted, *Música* 1, no. 11 (November 1920): 6–8.

Merino Montero, Luis. "Neuvas luces sobre Acario Cotapos." *Revista musical chilena* no. 159 (January–June 1983): 3–16.

———. "Cinco efemérides en la creación musical chilena." *Revista musical chilena* no. 167 (January–June 1987): 44–46.

Might's City Directories of Toronto, 1919–36.

Morey, Carl. "The Beginnings of Modernism in Toronto." In *Célébration: Essays on Aspects of Canadian Music,* ed. Godfrey Ridout and Talivaldis Kenins, 80–86. Toronto: Canadian Music Centre, 1984.

Neel, Boyd. "Alberto Guerrero." Royal Conservatory of Music *Monthly Bulletin,* January–February 1960, 1–2.

———. [abridged trans.] "Alberto García Guerrero juzgado por Boyd Neel," *Revista musical chilena* 70 (March–April 1960): 112–13

Oja, Carol. *Colin McPhee, Composer in Two Worlds.* Washington: Smithsonian Institution, 1990.

Orrego-Salas, Juan. "Exilio, ¿pérdida o provecho?" *Revista musical chilena* no. 199 (January–June 2003): 66–69.

Ortmann, Otto. *The Physiological Mechanics of Piano Technique.* London: K. Paul, Trench, Trubner, 1929.

Parker, William Belmont. *Chileans of To-day.* "Alberto García Guerrero," 391. Santiago: Hispanic Society of America, 1920. Reprint, New York: Kraus, 1967.

Pereira Salas, Eugenio. "La música chilena en los primeros cinquenta años del siglo XX." *Revista musical chilena* no. 40 (Summer 1950–51): 63–78.

Prado, Valeria Maino et al., eds. *Los Diez en el arte chileno del siglo XX.* Santiago: Editorial Universitaria, 1976.

Quiroga, Daniel. "Los hermanos García Guerrero." *Revista musical chilena* no. 2 (May 1946): 7–13.

Roberts, John, ed. *The Art of Glenn Gould: Reflections of a Musical Genius.* Toronto: Malcolm Lester, 1999.

Sadie, Stanley, ed. *The New Grove Dictionary of Music and Musicians.* London: Macmillan, 1980; 2nd ed. 2001.

———. *The New Grove Dictionary of Opera.* London: Macmillan, 1992.

Said, Edward W. *Musical Elabortions.* New York: Columbia University Press, 1991.

Salas Viú, Vicente. *La Creación musical en Chile, 1900–1951.* Santiago: Ediciones de la Universidad de Chile, n.d. [1952?].

Santa Cruz Wilson, Domingo. "Mis recuerdos sobre la Sociedad Bach." *Revista musical chilena* no. 40 (Summer 1950–51): 8–62.

Schmidl, Carlo, ed. *Supplemento al Dizionario universale dei musicisti.* Milan: Sozogno, n.d. [1938?].

Smith, Carleton Sprague. "The Composers of Chile." *Modern Music* 19, no. 1 (November–December 1941): 26–31.

Toronto Reference Library. Program files. "Guerrero, Alberto."

Trow's New York City Directory, 1917.

University of Toronto Archives. Toronto Conservatory of Music (after 1946, Royal Conservatory of Music), A-1975.

Uzcátegui García, Emilio. *Músicos chilenos contemporáneos: Datos biográficos e impresiones sobre sus obres.* Santiago: Imprento y Encuadernación América, 1919.

index

Bold numbers in the index indicate illustrations.